Anticipating the
Inevitable Changes
Coming to Canada

Anticipating the Inevitable Changes Coming to Canada

Preparing Canada and Canadians
for the 22nd Century

JAMES P. LUDWIG PH.D

Library of Congress Control Number:		2013904093
ISBN:	Hardcover	978-1-4836-0540-1
	Softcover	978-1-4836-0539-5
	Ebook	978-1-4836-0541-8

This book was printed in the United States of America.

Rev. date: 03/19/2013

To order additional copies of this book, contact:
Xlibris Corporation
1-888-795-4274
www.Xlibris.com
Orders@Xlibris.com
131020

CONTENTS

DEDICATION

This work is dedicated to Mike and (the late) June Gilbertson who introduced me to Alison Kilpatrick, setting me on the path to Canadian citizenship.

1

Where are we, where are we going and how fast?

CHANGE, DEATH AND taxes—three of the inevitable aspects of modern Canadian lives. Change may be the most difficult of these to grasp when we are in the midst of this continuous process. The 20th century revealed unprecedented changes of immense magnitude. In 1900, there were virtually no automobiles or trucks to move us, or our goods. There were no widespread means of communication outside of books, newspapers, telegraph and the earliest telephones to move ideas. Mean life spans were just above 50 years for North Americans. There were no antibiotics, nuclear weapons, airplanes or computers.

The changes of the last century were astonishing, so much so that a person alive in 1900 would not have recognized the world of 2000. Moreover, changes have accelerated in many areas to an astounding degree. Consider personal computers. In 1940, the closest things to computers were code machines, like the famous German *Enigma* of 1941. By the 1950s, IBM developed their UNIAC computer that required a three-story building, thousands of radio tubes and hundred of kilowatts of electric power to make computations. When the first lunar landing was accomplished in 1969, computers had advanced to transistor-powered units with about as much computational capacity as a Commodore 64, but were still state secrets. In the 1980s Apple, IBM and Microsoft brought forth the first personal computers. Today in 2013, I have on my desk a five year old MacBook Pro™ with ten thousand times the computing power of the lunar mission computers, an almost limitless access to software and programs and I am connected to virtually everyone I might wish to talk to through the Internet. Everything has changed in daily lives, and the pace of change will only accelerate in the 21st century. Change will be driven in part by ideas and entrepreneurs like the late Steve Jobs of Apple. But, change will also be influenced by trends and unique opportunities we have not seen, let alone thought about seriously.

Hindsight may allow us to develop perspective and insights about the changes we have experienced, but predicting how change will influence our societies is fraught with difficulties. Futurists have projected their views of how our societies will change for centuries—sometimes prescient, but more often projecting wildly inaccurate futures. Technology advances in bounds, often leapfrogging older technologies rapidly, rendering accepted concepts obsolete in just a few years. In the short term, every political campaign, marriage and individual's learning experience involves a projection of an anticipated future. We make decisions and act, expecting or hoping fervently for a particular outcome. Often, we are wildly inaccurate when we project a future for ourselves or country.

However, changes in the longer term, especially when driven by macro-scale trends individuals cannot control or influence meaningfully, are the grist of conjecture and often fiction. The responsible citizen must engage in the hard work of thinking about their future for their family, themselves, their country and the cultures in which they are embedded if there is to be any hope of altering the future beneficially when emerging or threatening trends are obvious. On the micro-level of our day-to-day lives, our choices of the way we Canadians live sum up the macro-direction of Canada.

So, where is Canada headed in the next nine decades that precede the 22nd century? More to the point, if we do not like the paths Canada and Canadians are on, or are being offered by our current political leaders, what can we do about it? Are there reasonable legal means available to us to alter course or to repair the inevitable deleterious effects of some past decisions or policies? If so, what are the likely long-term outcomes of various strategies and policies? Or, must we simply bow our heads, accepting meekly the changes that result from past human decisions, existing policies and the history of those geological accidents that formed the lands and waters that make up our nation?

JAMES P. LUDWIG PH.D

These are profound questions for Canadians since many believe that this is Canada's century to lead, excel and contribute greatly to human growth, even though the country does not have a strong reputation for leadership and innovation. If that is true, then Canadians have a great responsibility to consider their futures very carefully, for we Canadians could lead the world throughout the rest of this millennium if we make the best decisions soon.

Conversely, we could abdicate a leadership role to other nations and allow Canada's fate to be driven by others, most likely the Americans, Chinese and Indians. If so, the price we will pay is to lose our Canadian uniqueness. We will be forced adopt the values and political philosophies of others whether or not we like this fate. Arguably, this has already been the outcome of the last five decades for Canada. American values, political style campaigns, fast food, movies and economic philosophies have come to dominate much of Canada's landscape, businesses and culture. Are we, *should we*, be content with this outcome? Do we deserve to keep our distinct Canadian culture? If we believe we should strive to preserve Canada, then we have no choice but to shape our future by our Canadian interventions. This essay is about how we might do that and remain uniquely Canadian into the next century.

The North American Free Trade Agreement of 1988 (NAFTA) and the long-established International Joint Commission established by the Boundary Waters Treaty of 1909 set the stage for intensive cooperation and a closer economic union with the United States and Mexico in the 20th century. But, the events of September 11, 2001 (911) have gone a long way towards propelling all of North America, including Canada, into a fortress mentality at the behest of the Americans. Strong efforts are underway to develop a common North American border. Thus far, Canada has acquiesced to intense pressure from Americans to integrate border security between the two nations into a single effort, even though these actions smack of *de facto* surrender of Canadian autonomy.

Some thoughtful Canadians believe that this is the next step in a complete (possibly inevitable) political union between the US and Canada resulting in the total submersion of Canadian culture and values under the historic hegemony of the United States in North America. While that fear of creeping continentalism may seem somewhat paranoid and overblown, it is not unreasonable or inconsistent with the historic record. Given the extensive integration of the two economies, the emergence of the Canadian political right with its polarizing American style politics and the requirements under NAFTA to sell Canadian resources, particularly oil, preferentially to the US, our independent Canada is at genuine risk of being lost a bit at a time. In essence, Canada is being 'nibbled to death' by a modern form of old fashioned economic imperialism, mostly by the Americans and the Chinese.

The US has a long history of simply taking lands or control of resources by force or dictated treaties regardless of ownership. America fought wars with England, Mexico and Spain in the 19th Century to secure its present holdings, justifying its wars under the Monroe Doctrine that holds any actions in Western Hemisphere that may have any important impact on the US are open to US intervention. Considering the more recent Cuban Missile Crisis of 1961-62 and the US military interventions in Grenada, Nicaragua and Panama in the 1980s, the Monroe Doctrine is alive and well in the American psyche: It remains the lodestone of American foreign policy. Some would argue the two Iraq wars and the Afghan war of the last two decades are simply extensions of the Monroe Doctrine, undertaken and justified because airplanes, missiles and modern weapons of mass destruction eliminated the protection two vast oceans had afforded North America until well after World War II. Canadians would be incredibly naïve to think that the American Monroe Doctrine will never be adjusted and directed against Canada. If coercive actions against Canada are seen to be in the long-term interest of the Americans, it will be.

The 21st century will be a time when resources—particularly oil, natural gas, uranium and many strategic metals—become increasingly scarce and expensive. A dissection of the Canadian economy reveals Canada to be the largest supplier of oil, natural gas and forest products to the massive US economy. The export of just these three commodities contributed roughly 15% to the 1.737 trillion gross domestic product of Canada in 2010 (Statistics Canada). Substantial exports of electrical power, strategic metals, natural gas, other commodities and some manufactured goods flow south as well; over 85% of all Canadian exports went to the US in 2010.

As the largest trading partner of the US, the Canadian balance of payments and currency benefits greatly from these arrangements. However, a significant hidden price Canadians pay is buried inside historic infrastructure deficits. For example, there is no pan-Canadian oil or gas pipeline that unites the country with a secure energy distribution system *inside* Canada. Instead, most western Canadian oil and natural gas flows through pipelines that drop into the United States that removes upwards of two million barrels of oil and billions of cubic feet of gas per day for its voracious fossil fuel addiction.

What oil and gas is left then returns to Canada at Sarnia, Ontario and eastern Canada must buy some oil from foreign sources when the nation could supply all that Canadians use if a Canadian pipeline distribution system was sited only in Canada. Plans to increase the oil export rate to the US to well above two million barrels per day and construct new north:south pipelines are well underway. The most significant of these efforts is the Keystone pipeline addition to the Alberta network that will deliver an additional 800,000 barrels of Alberta oil sands heavy crude product to the gulf states' refineries in the US when the exact route is approved by US authorities.

Similarly, virtually the entire Canadian electric power grid is integrated north to south with the US grid; east to west connections are few and largely insignificant. In essence, Canadians trust Americans for their energy security. Although money flows north to pay for the exported resources at wholesale or discounted rates, especially for heavier grades of oil, America controls Canadian energy. Given the acquisitive history of the US for hegemonic control of North and South America by continued reliance on the Monroe Doctrine and the inevitable American hubris that mindset generates, such naive trust could be utterly misplaced when inevitable fossil fuel shortages occur again.

International cooperation, peacekeeping and good manners have long been the cornerstone Canadian values played out on the world stage. We have been a trusting generous people with a history of support for others under stress from both natural and man-made crises. Unlike the US, Canada has never sought to expand its borders, seize resources from others and rarely seeks to impose its political will on other nations by the use of military force. We have tried to lead quietly in international affairs by example—*until recently*. Until the Afghan war, Canadians' wars were always fought in support of 'mother' England, to protect Canada from the US in the 19th century or in internationally-sanctioned actions to protect innocent persons or cultures from aggression such as the Korean 'police action', Rwanda and the more recent efforts in Libya under the aegis of the United Nations and NATO.

The question really comes down to this—Can the United States be trusted to respect Canadian laws and sovereignty when other Canadian policies and ways of dealing with Canadian citizens' needs (like health care and taxation) diverge substantially from US law or policies? Is the United States the benign 'good neighbor Uncle Sam' to the south who will respect Canadian sovereignty no matter what occurs and when material shortages develop in the US that Canada can supply? Or, is Uncle Sam really a rapacious economic predator dressed in the sheep's clothing of legitimate businessmen awaiting only the right moment and naïve Canadian political allies to pounce upon, and then dismember Canada in order to obtain unfettered access to Canada's resources? Or does the genuine intent of the US political leaders towards Canada lie somewhere in between these two extreme views?

Is the possible 'forced marriage' of the two nations in the best interests of Canadians? My short answer is no—*an unequivocal no at that*. This essay explores why I hold this opinion, the historical and cultural histories than influence both nations and then offers strategies and ideas to assure the survival of Canada and Canadian values into the 22nd Century. Many readers may find it odd that a native-born American would come to write this long essay. However, as a dual US-Canadian citizen born in a border city (Port Huron, Michigan), I worked for thirty-seven years as an ecological researcher on colonial water bird populations of the jointly-managed Great Lakes, consulted with government agencies and corporations on ecological matters on both sides of the border for 42 years, married a Canadian and became a Canadian citizen. I have had an unusually intimate view of the two countries with their distinct histories and cultures from a unique working perspective over a seventy-one year life. I am arrogant enough to believe (as a typical American would) that I have both a unique and valuable perspective to offer all Canadians—native and naturalized citizens alike.

JAMES P. LUDWIG PH.D

I have also had experiences of work with government agencies and many professionals in both nations. These experiences provided both the time and extensive opportunities to assess the differences in governmental attitudes, citizens' values and cultures of the two countries in many settings. Since the experience of 911, the unbridled American military response and the economic crises of the 2008-2012 period have destabilized the world fundamentally in the last decade. A reactive, morally deficient military and economic underbelly of the American character, foreign policy and economy has been exposed for all to see. It is crucial that Canadians to explore these issues fully now. For, if Canadians wait to 'see what happens', it could very well be far too late to influence the policies of Canadian governments leading us ever closer to economic and *de facto* political union with the United States.

The recent drift of Canadian politics into American style political campaigns with confrontational rhetoric and vicious *ad hominem* attack ads demands that Canadians think through the implications of close cooperation with, and adherence to, American values before the essence of Canada is lost forever. Even though I was born an American and only came to Canadian citizenship late in life, I would mourn that fate for Canada deeply—as should all thoughtful Canadians and those Americans who support those universal lofty values of fairness, equity, opportunity and freedom inscribed in the American Declaration of Independence and Constitution. A fundamental reason to explore these issues today is the all to obvious departure from many these honorable traditional American values in the last three decades by American leaders. Americans and Canadians have a profound need to understand why these changes have happened, and how to restore a defensible ethical balance, especially within America. How these issues are resolved is incredibly important to the citizens of both nations.

Canadians have a profound need to contemplate carefully the relationship of Canada to the United States in order to preserve an independent Canada as we know it. Then, we must act on our carefully thought out conclusions.

2

The distinct cultures of two North American nations.

T HE LAST HALF of the 18th and first half of the 19th centuries were periods of great political uncertainty in North America. The resolution of two centuries of French-English conflict over which colonial power would dominate the 'New World' occurred between 1755 and 1763 with the French and Indian Wars in the American colonies and the defeat of the French on the Plains of Abraham in Quebec in 1759. These events were followed just two decades later with the American colonists' uprisings in New England culminating in the American Revolution, the military defeat of England in 1783 and the official formation of the United States of America in 1789. However, military conflicts between the English-controlled Upper Canada and the United States persisted until the War of 1812 boiled over following US attempts to evict English Loyalists from Upper Canada (now Ontario) and expand the US borders to the north. The 1814 Treaty of Ghent largely ratified the pre-1812 borders of America and Upper Canada from Maine and New Brunswick as far west as Lake Superior. But, border disputes would continue for another seven decades in the west as American Northwest was settled.

Between the US presidential elections of 1844 and 1872, the boundary issues of western Canada and Oregon territory simmered relentlessly until the 49th parallel agreement and the ownership of the Juan de Fuca Channel islands between Washington and British Columbia finally settled the northwest border of the US as the 49th parallel. Much of the outcome and contentiousness of US-Canada boundary disputes in the 19th century was the aftermath of the way the American Revolution separated the thirteen American colonies from Great Britain by force that divided most North Americans into two armed hostile camps of American revolutionaries or Canadian loyalists to 'mother' England. Predictably, a half-dozen generations passed before the sharp memories of these armed conflicts subsided. Many modern Canadians descended from British loyalists who settled Ontario and fought for Upper Canada in the War of 1812 still retain a culturally inherited wariness about the intent and character of Americans, and well they should.

During the 19th century the fundamental political underpinnings of US foreign and domestic policy emerged, largely owing to the heavy-handed colonial policies of Great Britain, France and Spain and American fears over new European invasions of the Americas. On the one hand, the Monroe Doctrine emerged as a cornerstone of American foreign policy in the 1823 presidential State of the Union address to Congress. President Monroe included this statement that defined this most important permanent cornerstone of American foreign policy:

> ". . . . the occasion has been judged proper for asserting as a principle in which the rights and interests of the United States are involved, that the American continents, by the free and independent condition which they have assumed and maintained, are henceforth not to be considered as subjects for future colonization by any European powers."

On the other hand, US domestic policy for North America in the 19th century was driven by a vision of 'Manifest Destiny' that would see the borders of the US extended from the Atlantic to Pacific Oceans. The US attempted to seize and annex parts of what is now Canada first in the war of 1812 and periodically for the next 60 years, particularly in the west along what is now the British Columbia—Alberta borders with Washington, Idaho and Montana. The infamous phrase "54° 40' or fight" (the north latitude claimed by the American expansionists) figured in numerous US politicians' campaigns in the mid-1800s until the American Civil War deflected American's attention to internal issues. Only then was the stage set to resolve the long-standing disputes over the location of the western US-Canada border, largely to the 49th parallel.

During the 19th century some US lands were purchased from European powers, notably the Louisiana and Alaska purchases from France and

Russia, respectively. Others were seized in the Mexican War (California, New Mexico, Arizona, Nevada, Texas). Still other lands (notably Cuba and the Philippine Islands) were seized in the Spanish American War and ruled as colonial protectorates before being established as independent nations in the 20th century. A few other islands in the Caribbean Ocean remain US possessions, particularly Puerto Rico and the US Virgin Islands. Hawaii, Guam and a few other islands in the Pacific Ocean round out the modern US holdings. In retrospect, it is noteworthy just how much of the United States was seized by the application of brute military force under the Monroe Doctrine. Substantially, America decreed the Americas to be their sphere of influence and has dared any nation to challenge that assertion almost two centuries.

The political-cultural legacy of the decision to separate from, or remain loyal to, Great Britain still resonates in politics of the two nations today—the US with the republic model of democracy, Canada with the British parliamentary model. Similarly, other fundamental differences in attitudes of citizens in the two nations persist into the 21st century. Fundamental Canadian attitudes and values show little sign of changing in spite of the importation of many aspects of American culture (Adams 2003). The present system of cooperation to prevent pollution of boundary waters and provide for joint management to prevent damage to these resources by the US and Canada was not established until the Boundary Waters Treaty was negotiated by Great Britain with the United States on behalf of the British commonwealth nation of Canada in 1909. Canadian attitudes toward other nations still resonate to the original decisions of pre-Confederation Canadians to remain both conservatively loyal to England, and to interfere in the decisions or effect changes to other nation's policies by force only rarely. Afghan policies since 2003 are a notable and troubling exception to this historic Canadian foreign policy of non-involvement in foreign wars that do not affect the Commonwealth or Canada directly.

In sharp contrast, American policy has held for nearly two centuries that it has the right to interfere preemptively with other nations' policies and actions, whenever US interests are believed to be at stake in the Western Hemisphere. In the 20th Century, the Cuban Missile Crisis, the invasion of Grenada, the Iran-Contra Affair involving Nicaragua and the police action to arrest Noriega in Panama all were manifestations of the same

JAMES P. LUDWIG PH.D

adherence to the Monroe Doctrine—sometimes disguised, sometimes overtly displayed. In the 21st century, the Second Gulf and Afghan Wars are the cultural legacy of the American imperial superpower following the same pugnacious foreign policy it began with in the revolutionary war nearly 250 years earlier, then perfected as the Monroe Doctrine and Manifest Destiny. The military justification for these actions was the Monroe Doctrine, now extended back to the 'Old World' on the questionable basis that distance and the presence of the formerly effective oceanic barriers to possible enemies are no longer as significant or an effective protection as they once were.

It was especially revealing to have listened closely to the rhetoric from US politicians in the Bush administration in the lead up to the Second Gulf (Iraq) War. Carefully crafted, boldly inaccurate justifications were offered for implementing the same old American foreign policies of the last two centuries. The 'new' *Axis of Evil* enemies, particularly Iraq, in the Middle East were said to have had weapons of mass destruction that could reach North America, uranium stockpiles, the technology for making nuclear bombs and that they had harbored Al-Queda terrorists before 911. None of those assertions were true of Iraq, although the Taliban in Afghanistan did have prominent ties to the Al Queda terrorists. Once the press exposed these systematic lies, the American politicians switched tacks boldly to claim the real reason was to spread democracy to the Iraqi people and dethrone a dictator. Interestingly, the Bush Administration actually reduced military efforts to the minimum in Afghanistan where Al Queda remained entrenched with their Taliban allies after 2003 as the US military focused on Iraq. But, American leaders avoided most carefully any mention of control of Iraq's substantial oil reserves. All this suggests that the true justification for the Second Gulf War was to support a military operation designed to secure access to Iraqi oil reserves and that it had very little to do with either 911 or replacing a foul dictator for ethical reasons.

However, in the context of the Monroe Doctrine and the long history of similar fallacious reasoning by many US administrations for two hundred years in support of various wars and military actions, this was neither a new or unique tactic to justify the use of American military force. Rather, the Monroe Doctrine, merely massaged and adapted for Iraq and Afghanistan was the same old 'tried and true' policy for North America shrouded in a cloak of deceptive modern rhetoric. The first decade of the 21st century has merely confirmed that the US has not grown beyond its historic reach for absolute control of the Western Hemisphere and anyone who *might* attempt to influence what happens there. In the American view, everything in the Western Hemisphere must be subordinated to US interests. Importantly, now that the doctrine has been extended worldwide with the United States acting as the world's 'policeman', one must conclude that no sovereign nation is exempt from US attack. Make no mistake, that conclusion now includes Canada. Moreover, this behavior can only fuel a simmering distrust of American motives by thoughtful people in many other nations.

As Canadians, we must be aware of the pervasive and fundamental nature of the long established American worldview and policy construct simply because Canada is the largest and most resource-rich part of North America. Since Canadian Confederation in 1867 Americans have used diplomacy, treaties, investments and economic clout to get what they have wanted from Canada. Mexico, Cuba, Panama, various Caribbean and other Central and South American nations have been far less fortunate, often facing invasions by the overwhelming force of American Marines. If we are to be prudent protectors of Canada's future, as Canada exceeds the US in per capita wealth (which seems inevitable), develops its strategic resources (particularly oil, uranium and other minerals), continues to have a publicly-funded reasonably cost-effective health care system that produces greater life spans for its citizens (>2 years more than Americans) and has a superior life experience based on a multicultural view of the world, prudence alone demands that we must ask the unthinkable 'Are we next?'

Should Canadians expect the war of 1812 to be refought over Canadian resources, lands and policies? Suppose Canada sells resources Americans covet to China, Russia or another nation the US regards as unfriendly or suspect. How then will the Americans seek to impose their will on Canada—by negotiation, rhetoric and treaties negotiated without coercion? Or will America default to brute military or gross economic force as it has done to so many other nations in the Western Hemisphere and more recently elsewhere in the 'Old World' for the last two centuries?

What seems certain is that America will seek to impose its will on Canada for the fundamental doctrines of American foreign policy and the

JAMES P. LUDWIG PH.D

political myths Americans believe in support of their hubris and views are embedded in the very marrow of the US political skeleton and grey matter of the American psyche. As the only true superpower measured by military might and a two century old track record of defaulting to the use of military force to secure land and resources, the temptation to use military force is always a viable option to US presidents. Neither leopards, nor American presidents, are likely to change their spots, bedrock foreign policies or hunting techniques anytime soon.

What Canadians must face up to is that their relations with America and Americans in the 21st century are likely to evolve to become far more rancorous than was the relatively cooperative and benign relationship of the 20th century. What this reality means for Canada and Canadians remains to be seen. But, it cannot be ignored safely.

3

The inevitable 21st Century trends driving change in Canada.

C ANADA AND THE entire world face a set of trends and changes this century that accelerated during the late 20th century into serious worldwide stressors. Among these are seven realities: explosive world population growth, diminished food security, tight energy supplies, increasingly scarce raw materials, decline in quality and quantities of fresh water, rapid climate change and religious/political fundamentalism of many stripes. Canada seems relatively immune from some of these trends (e.g. energy and raw material supplies) owing to various internal factors affording the nation a large degree of insulation from the worst impacts of those trends. But Canada is as much hostage to other troubling trends as any other nation, especially climate change, degrading fresh water quality and religious fundamentalism.

Canada has relatively very few people (34 million in 2011, about 0.48 percent of the world's burgeoning population of seven billion) for its land area and resources (the second largest nation in land area). Various projections of the world population have settled in at an estimated nine to ten billion people alive in 2050, rising to about 12 billion by 2100; that could be the upper limit of the planet's carrying capacity for the human species. There is intense interest among many foreign nationals, particularly well-educated professionals, to become Canadians for good reason. The country is democratic with a strong economy, many opportunities, a history of multiculturalism with two official languages, universal health care and a well-deserved reputation as a welcoming society that does not impose cultural limits or force integration on its immigrant citizens.

In this regard, Canadian attitudes of multiculturalism towards immigrants are very distinct from the American 'melting pot' and one official (English) language approach. American leaders and the American culture seek to homogenize all immigrants into the English-speaking cultural model as the only acceptable path towards full acceptance in the United States. Canadians also have a far more liberal and accepting view of people and their needs than do most Americans. The universal Canadian health care system, extended parental leave, unfettered abortion rights, less divisive politics and a much less influential fundamentalist Christian religious right are a few of the distinguishing differences that make Canada attractive to a wide diversity of immigrants.

This is especially so for those not steeped in the Christian fundamentalist culture of America that is vociferous, pugnacious and very engaged in American politics. Several authors, perhaps most pointedly Chris Hedges, have even explored the role of Christian fundamentalism of the American Right as a covert war on American values, dangerously close to fascism in content, methods and philosophy (Hedges 2006). Indeed, there is a remarkable—even scary—similarity of rhetoric and treatment of women between fundamentalist Christian sects and the rigid thinking of the fundamentalist Muslim Taliban of Central Asian. Hedges summed up the similarities this way:

> *"It is perhaps telling that our (America's) closest allies in the United Nations on issues dealing with reproductive rights, one of the of issues where we (Americans) cooperate with other nations, are Islamic states such as Iran. But, then the Christian Right and radical Islamists, although locked in a holy war, increasingly mirror each other. They share the same obsessions. They do not tolerate other forms of belief or disbelief. They are at war with artistic and cultural expression. They seek to silence the media. They call for subjugation of women. They promote sexual repression and they seek to express themselves through violence."* (Hedges 2006).

Americans tend to 'talk the talk' on issues of human rights, tolerance and equality while most Canadians 'walk the walk' and expect to enjoy the freedoms and dignities these human rights embody in day to day contexts. That said, some of these rights (e.g. abortion, privacy) are under continuous attack even in Canada, largely from the Canadian political right and Christian fundamentalists. With much of the media of both countries willing to give coverage to fundamentalists in the name of 'balanced reporting', the seductive messages of the Christian Right fomenting fear and then offering simplistic solutions, an inexorable slide into fascism seems quite possible in both countries. Fortunately, Canada seems much less likely to slip into this kind of degradation of human rights and thereby remains far more attractive to those people willing to tolerate those who embrace beliefs and ideas they do not. Substantially, Canadian multiculturalism is a significant coat of armor against the fascist-like intolerance lurking in America.

Taken together, these are all factors that make Canada an exceptionally attractive destination for political, cultural and climate refugees as well as immigrants from other nations, especially the better-educated and wealthier potential immigrants from less fortunate nations. In essence, this translates to Canada having the opportunity to pick the best, brightest and wealthiest immigrants from the greater potential pool of candidates throughout the 21st century. A well-crafted immigration policy can ensure that many of the best immigrants available become new Canadians.

Given the fact that native-born Canadians do not produce enough babies (2.3 children/couple) even to maintain the current population stable, Canadian population maintenance and growth will have to be met through immigration. Selecting the best educated to become Canadians will assure a top quality work force and an innovative populace. By selecting wealthier candidates, Canada can also enjoy a form of gross domestic product growth increase simply by admitting persons with money to spend and invest here.

Food security is a perpetual problem throughout the third world and even in a few developed nations. Food security depends on having sufficient arable land with adequate fertility, rainfall, crop storage capability and an effective food distribution network. Canada is blessed with a surfeit of all five factors. Canada is a world-leader in production for export of wheat, lentils, canola, beef and other agricultural products, exporting large volumes of these food commodities to other nations. While droughts and floods occur from time to time limiting some regional Canadian harvests occasionally, Canada is a leading exporter of crop and fertilizer commodities consistently. Further, much arable land is presently fallowed or not used for crops, especially in the Maritimes, northern Ontario and even the Prairie provinces.

JAMES P. LUDWIG PH.D

As the world population and international demand for reliable sources of food grows, especially with global warming associated with rapid climate change, Canada can increase its agricultural production immensely without sacrificing lands or rare ecosystems. In fact, where global climate change will devastate agriculture in many places (e.g. north Africa, the Russian steppes and central Asia), Canadian agriculture is far more likely to benefit from warmer temperatures, longer growing seasons and generally increased precipitation associated with a warmer climate. Food security *per se* is not likely to be a problem for Canadians in this century, although food quality, poorly-regulated pesticide use, food additives, and related issues like genetically-modified plants will continue to be issues for Canadians owing to the capture of Canada's health and environmental regulatory agencies by corporate interests (Chopra, 2009).

Canada has very large reserves of energy commodities including gas, oil, uranium, coal and hydroelectric, and also has immense potential to foster and develop renewable energies, especially wind and tidal energy. In general, Canada produces far more raw fossil fuel energy commodities that can be used in Canada and exports the vast majority of this domestic surplus to the United States, particularly oil and natural gas. Presently, Canada is the largest supplier of oil and second largest source of foreign natural gas for the United States. Roughly, 12 percent of the total value ($101 billion USD) of all Canadian exports was due to these two fossil fuel commodities sent to the United States in 2010 (Statistics Canada). Hydroelectric energy and metallurgical coal exports together provide roughly five percent of the value of all exports. Exports of energy commodities, most to the US, accounted for more than one-fifth of the total of Canada's balance of payments, and nearly 10% of Canada's gross domestic product in 2009.

Most of the money exchanged for these commodities comes from the United States. With energy escalating in value as worldwide scarcities develop, these energy commodities may soon come to account for one-third or even more of the Canadian balance of payments and more than a sixth of the nation's GDP. This fortunate largesse underpins the Canadian dollar and economy in a fundamental manner.

Other commodities, especially dimension lumber, added-value forestry products, potash and various mineral and mined products form another large piece of the Canadian export and domestic economy. Thus far, the sheer volume of forested land in Canada has guaranteed that the forestry sector has available a very large standing timber supply for harvest, far more than is used in Canada. There are local shortages of timber, significant forest damage from invasive insects in many regions and the unknown of how boreal Canadian forests will respond to rapid climate change. However, significant damage to boreal pine and spruce forests is one probable outcome of climate change and invasive insect species. More southern and alien insect species that could devastate conifers in our northern boreal forests must be expected to arrive, survive and prosper. Some alien insects, like the pine bark beetle and emerald ash borer, are already causing serious damage to standing timber.

Although mining has been an important part of the Canadian landscape and economy for nearly 150 years, recent exploration and new mines have revealed just how little of this largesse has been found and brought into production. With the world's largest known potash reserves, huge heavy oil and coal reserves, substantial uranium deposits, gold, silver, nickel, cobalt, copper, diamonds, rare earths, platinum group metals in the Canadian Shield and other important minerals scattered across the country from the Arctic Circle to the southern border, Canada is among the most self-sufficient of all nations in minerals. Global climate change, especially rising worldwide temperatures, will probably benefit most mining developments in the north by making access easier, provided there are substantial investments in transportation infrastructure in the Canadian north. A completely new, but very expensive, transportation infrastructure will be required wherever the permafrost melts and mines are developed.

Thus far, many of Canada's mineral deposits have been developed, often with funds invested from foreign sources and then traded on world commodity markets. Of all sectors of the Canadian economy, mining has evolved from regional/national Canadian-owned enterprises into a part of the worldwide economy. The purchase and mergers of many Canadian 'juniors' and even larger iconic Canadian mining firms like International Nickel and Falconbridge by the largest multinational companies transformed Canadian mining into a modest piece of the worldwide mining sector. BHP-Billiton, Rio Tinto and Vale among the huge multinational mining firms have swallowed up numerous smaller Canadian companies in the last twenty years, to the chagrin of many thoughtful Canadians. The same pattern has emerged with energy companies suggesting a thorough review of Canadian policies towards mining and energy, especially the degree of foreign ownership and control of these sectors, is long overdue.

Abundant fresh water has been a Canadian strength since confederation, although our water policies often seem to be wasteful and ill conceived. Joint US-Canada control of 20% of the world's fresh water in the Great Lakes is under the control of each nation's regulatory agencies and overseen by the International Joint Commission. The IJC is charged with the responsibility to oversee the effectiveness of the two governments' laws, regulations and to advise on border water use issues. However, Canada and the US have managed the border water issues between the two nations with very modest success. The joint failure to prevent pervasive toxic substances pollution and invasions by a host of damaging alien species, especially in the Great Lakes, has exposed how vulnerable Canada's immense fresh water resources are. Sadly, the prospects for improvements in fresh water management are poor as North American neoliberal governments withdraw support from environmental regulatory agencies in both countries.

Aerial pollutant transport of toxic substances from worldwide sources threatens to degrade Canadian waters even more seriously, especially arctic region water quality (Visser 2007). Global temperature increases are depleting important mountain glaciers in Canada, particularly in Alberta, at an astonishing rate. Because these glaciers have supplied much of the fresh waters available to Alberta and Saskatchewan (roughly 40% of the annual flows of the Bow and Athabasca Rivers), these provinces are on the cusp of a serious, even economically debilitating, fresh water supply and quality crisis. All sorts of domestic and mining related uses depend on these waters, especially fresh water for the domestic needs of Calgary and Edmonton and industrial process waters for oil sands developments.

The mining and upgrading of the oil sands is one cause of serious degradation of Lake Athabasca's water quality owing to both airborne and point-source discharges of oil field and oil sands pollutants, chemicals and especially salt. Lake Athabasca seems destined to be transformed into a saline lake and lose many freshwater species. Aboriginal Cree communities have suffered great disruptions to traditional ways and quality of life from these developments in the last two decades. Understanding exactly what a 40% reduction in the annual water supply of these regions will mean and responding effectively must be one of the top Canadian water policy priorities for the first half of the 21st Century.

Ancillary issues on water supply and quality include how much more hydroelectric power should be developed, especially in British Colombia, Quebec and Newfoundland & Labrador. The three Arctic territories face the impending loss of permafrost, vastly accelerated erosion, soil instabilities (particularly solifluction) and very different surface water and groundwater dynamics as patterns of precipitation and seasonality change rapidly. Canadians cannot be certain that these threats will be managed well with current national and provincial policies. This is especially true with the wholesale layoff of many Canadian scientists, shutdown of programs like the large lakes research program, and the propensity of the Harper government to discredit their own scientists.

The North American Free Trade Agreement may well be a serious impediment to the development of wise Canadian water policies by *de facto* usurpation of Canadian autonomy to address these issues, and the relentless exploitation of Canadian mineral and energy resources for, and by, offshore interests. Canadians should understand that developing these resources always requires access to fresh water and that the availability of water is the most likely limiting factor for many natural resource developments. Canada cannot depend upon, and Canadians must not assume, that limitless supplies of useable freshwater will be present in the future.

Political-religious fundamentalism is a rising worldwide problem that swirls darkly beneath an apparently calm surface in Canada. This is not a new or unique phenomenon. It has recurred regularly for thousands of years cyclically, often in response to religious wars and reactionary political/religious movements. Canadian multiculturalism tends to ameliorate this problem to some degree, but many ethnic groups, especially Christian and Muslim fundamentalists, and individuals flirt with (or harbor) notions that their politics and religion (often in bizarre mixtures) have been ordained as the only correct path by a supreme being. Worse, some zealots extend this claim of moral superiority to justifications for violence, as the Air India incident in 1986 showed Canadians graphically. Canada will not be immune from this kind of terrorism and violence.

To a large extent, dealing with this problem offshore—as the United States has done for two centuries through application of their Monroe Doctrine—is the pathway Canada was induced (or coerced) to follow to enter into the Afghan War. Many argue that attempting to suppress fundamentalism by force abroad simply breeds a more intense version of it. Worse, it may attract those who practice radical fundamentalism to bring their ideas and acts of violence covertly into Canada in retaliation for Canadian support of American foreign policy. If so, that could induce Canadians to react with military force as the Americans have done should there be a substantial terrorist attack in Canada. Recent Canadian policies are akin to a child kicking the hornet's nest.

Whether military force can contain fundamentalist religious extremism is an open question. America has been successful only when overwhelming force was used, while civilian casualties ('collateral damage') and the important question of whether military force would only provoke more intense anti-western reactions and terrorism were ignored. Moreover, the deployment of military force against persons, organizations or regimes that have been demonized as different, or as imagined threats (as happened with Iraq in 2003), does nothing to alleviate the paranoia and restive actions of those already in Canada. Neither can military action defeat persons and overseas organizations that harbor uncompromising notions of moral or religious superiority.

There is no doubt that this kind of political/religious fundamentalism will be present throughout the 21st century, partly because people in poor or oppressed nations gravitate toward the simple certainty blind faith in traditional religious or political doctrines offers for their problems, especially in times of stress and crisis. Culturally and historically, Canadian multiculturalism may offer a far better means to deal with this problem effectively than does the American choice to employ massive military forces in order to subjugate those perceived to be external enemies, or the inherent threats of home-grown terrorists.

4

Inevitable worldwide physical trends and unforeseeable events.

THERE ARE MANY events and trends worldwide that Canadian policies and actions influence only slightly (e.g. global climate change); others like earthquakes, tsunamis, volcanic eruptions, large weather events, etc. must be expected but are beyond human control or prediction. When and where these natural events will happen is unknowable. At best, we can only plan, position resources and be ready to respond to these disasters that will happen. For some regions, historic weather records and geological knowledge are very helpful to show about where, and with an approximate frequency, these debilitating natural events can be expected. Tornados are frequent events in the mid-continental provinces, hurricanes or typhoons in the coastal provinces, but rare elsewhere. Geological faults and crustal plate movements identify particular regions, like British Colombia, as prone to earthquakes and volcanism.

Coastal areas, particularly British Colombia, are subject to tsunamis from earthquakes that occur half the world away in the oceanic basins. Although the east coast of Canada has not experienced such a catastrophic event in several centuries, nonetheless it is still vulnerable as there are unstable faults at the continental margins of Europe and Africa that could cause large tsunami events in the Atlantic. As the 2004 Christmas earthquake in Indonesia and 2011 earthquake and tsunami in Japan demonstrated vividly, when tsunamis occur, the damage can be swift, immense and calamitous. Even worldwide markets suffer when damage from these events coincides with important global resources, commodities or industrial capacity.

Canada has one great stable geological asset amongst the earth's continental plates that insulates the heart of the nation somewhat from these instabilities—the great Canadian Shield. The shield is one of the most stable geological regions on earth. Where many other nations are underlain mostly by either moving continental plates or well-faulted younger sedimentary rocks prone to earthquakes, the shield is essentially one great piece of stable crust made of ancient metamorphic and volcanic rocks with relatively few faults, little tendency to move or have any appreciable earthquakes. The shield is the anchor of the North American continent. It is almost entirely contained in Canada where it is exposed at the surface. It consists mostly of very hard erosion resistant rocks that are ancient, having withstood many glaciations and the relentless forces of erosion for 1.5 to 3.8 billion years. The oldest shield rocks date almost to the earliest time of the planet's formation. Many places on the shield also host valuable minerals.

The primary disadvantage to the shield region of Canada is minimal soil. Much of the soil that had developed on the shield since the Cretaceous period was scoured off by the four Pleistocene glaciations that moved most of the better mineral soils far to the south into the prairie provinces, southern Ontario and the northern United States. Shield soils are usually very thin, acidic and nutrient-poor leaving the region less suited to agriculture and somewhat hostile to development activities that benefit from access to large amounts of soils such as buried pipelines. These properties make the shield well suited for projects that require very stable conditions such as mines or nuclear power plants. It is insulated from ground motion, severe coastal storms, tsunamis and has a small human population making the region suitable for many inherently dangerous developments.

Further, the shield is an ecological region dominated now by boreal forests and taiga that will experience rapid catastrophic ecological upsets accompanying climate change. Completely new ecologies will invade the Canadian north in the next 100 years. The boreal forests and permafrost ecologies we see, protect and enjoy today will not be present where they now are by the 22nd century. This fact should initiate great consternation among environmentalists because any decisions to protect particular biotic resources now present at a given location will be valid no longer. Simple decisions to set aside tracts of land or ocean floor for particular biological communities will be sabotaged by climate change altering basic conditions rapidly.

By the end of this century, the ecologies of the Arctic and near arctic regions will be in the throes of very fast and fundamental changes. Considerable volumes of clean fresh water are stored at the surface of the shield in bedrock depressions as lakes and *Sphagnum*-dominated peat bogs. The existing tree cover is often the taiga and boreal forest types dominated by low diversity black spruce associations. In the northern regions near and above the Arctic Circle the taiga forests give way to muskeg dominated by shrubs and mosses. These arctic plant associations were usually underlain with permafrost, but many regions are already experiencing permafrost melting leading to collapsing forest associations ('drunken trees'), excessive and large methane releases and very unstable organic soils prone to liquify and erode when the permafrost melts.

Excessive methane releases will follow permafrost melting. Methane releases are a very prominent positive feedback mechanism to rapid—even runaway—global climate change following on the worldwide temperature increase. Methane is at least 20 fold more effective a greenhouse gas than carbon dioxide and eventually is photo-oxidized to carbon dioxide in the atmosphere. Ecologically, the northern margins of the Canadian Shield host the most vulnerable of all Canada's ecosystems. Species like the polar bear, many migratory shorebirds and the characteristic plants of the taiga and shrub-scrub areas dependant on permafrost, or those depend on sea ice floes, are being lost at astonishing rates. Most likely, there is little Canadians can do to prevent the loss of many of these populations. Many species' extinctions were outcomes of historic fast climate change as will be new patterns of migrations and attempts to adapt by iconic animal species.

Simply designating these lands as ecological reserves or parks cannot protect these ecologies. Canadians, particularly rabid environmentalists bent on protection of *'our true north wild and free'*, will have to face up to the reality that their romanticized visions of these ecologies and integral to our Canadian myth system will be devastated as climate change proceeds. The primary tool of our noble conservation movements has been to designate lands in perpetuity as parks and reserves in order to protect particular species and intact ecologies of concern. But, this strategy rests squarely upon the assumption that climate and climate effects on ecologies will not change substantially for the designated area and its denizens. For example, Canada has a park on Hudson Bay established specifically for the protection and conservation of polar bears, a species that depends on sea ice for survival. It is an open question if this iconic species can survive as sea ice disappears. If the polar bear fails to adapt to the new reality, does a polar bear national reserve without sea ice make any sense where it is now? Most regrettably, the answer is no, although a park at the same site for other species that come to occupy this area may make perfect conservation sense.

Permafrost loss will likely cause little direct economic damage in the north except to coastal communities. But, those businesses and communities that rely on frozen lakes and permafrost to provide secure winter transportation will suffer as their supply chains are interrupted. Very importantly, permafrost loss will expose the Canadian north as grossly deficient in developed infrastructure including roads, electric power, pipelines, airports, seaports and railroads. Immense investments will be required to bring this region into high economic productivity in a much warmer Canada. For the remainder of this century, Canadians should expect to see enormous dislocations to the aboriginal cultures and ecosystems of the north, bringing devastation to traditional life styles, but great opportunity as well. Whether this situation is well managed or bungled will go a long way toward defining the success of Canada and all Canadians in the 22nd century and beyond. These changes will be the greatest challenge to the leadership of all levels of governments, including the First Nations, in this century.

Climate change, specifically global temperature increases, will drive these nearly cataclysmic changes in the north. Some impacts, notably those to agriculture and a more ready access to northern Canada that the recent cold climates have long denied will likely be net benefits. However, equally large but more gradual changes, will be experienced in the developed southern regions of Canada; many of these impacts will be negative. Invasions of many southern weeds, animals, pests, animal and human parasites that winter cold had eliminated are inevitable. While some crop plants that cannot be grown now in Canada will become viable crops for Canadian farmers, parts of the country may well experience serious droughts, especially some of the provinces in the rain shadow of the Rocky Mountains, the prairie provinces and the Great Lakes. Some of these areas have been projected to lose 4-8% of their annual water supply from rainfall and experience a 6-8% increased water loss owing to heightened rates of evaporation and plant transpiration as temperatures rise and growing seasons lengthen. What is clear is that both groundwater recharge and runoff will decrease and that will damage agriculture and ground water supplies.

For example, if the Great Lakes are to be maintained as transportation corridor either massive dredging or large outflow restrictions could be required to maintain current water levels. Degraded water quality, especially owing to the potent toxins produced by blue-green algae, will become common in the Great Lakes and many inland lakes. Algal degradation of water quality may well become the most significant water quality problem of all inland freshwater lakes similar to the toxic conditions that are common to many African lakes and a major cause of unsafe drinking water there. *Per capita* electrical energy use and demands in summer will increase dramatically. Air quality, especially in Ontario, Quebec and the Maritimes, will suffer from much greater rates of summertime ozone formation.

However, it is the Canadian seacoasts that will experience the most fundamental disruptions by the end of this century from climate change. Consider these facts: The first official international science-based climate change panel (IPCC) projections of global seal level rise for the 21st century done in the late 1980s projected a maximum worldwide sea level rise of 25 cm ±10 cm by 2100 and a 1° C average temperature increase worldwide. Subsequently, there have been six revisions to these forecasts, the latest of which is the current estimate of 100-150 cm and + 3° C by 2100. The most recent comprehensive data indicates a global temperature increase of 1.1° C has already occurred, already exceeding the original estimate for the next 110 years made 25 years ago. Every projection based on the best available science and data at the moment the projection was done has been a sizeable increase in the projected magnitude and rate of global temperatures and sea level rise during the 21st century. Crucially, there is no end in sight to the increasing *rate* of the projected sea level rise. Moreover, no one has determined just how great the total rise in ocean levels could be, largely because we do not yet know where global temperatures will stabilize from man-induced warming.

JAMES P. LUDWIG PH.D

The volume of water stored in the now rapidly melting Greenland ice sheet *alone* can raise global sea level by 600 ± 50 cm (> 19 feet). The volumes of water stored in melting tropical and temperate zone mountain glaciers will add another 40-55 cm, and that now stored in Arctic permafrost will add another 20-50 cm. These dire estimates do not account for either the thermal expansion of the oceans as they warm nor any melting contributed from the vast landed Antarctic ice sheet. A global sea level rise by the mid-22nd century in the 7-10 meter range is reasonable to anticipate; rather, this catastrophic degree of change is very likely and could be even greater.

Few Canadians know that during warmer late Miocene and early Pliocene time (~ 5 million years ago), global oceans were 17 and 27 meters higher than today in two episodes (URL:http://3dparks.wr.usgs.gov/nyc/coastalplain/coastalplain.htm). Greenland, much of the Arctic and some of the Antarctic were substantially ice-free then. In the Eocene (about 55 million years ago) when Arctic and Antarctic were warm, there was no water trapped in ice at either pole, global sea levels were about 220 feet (67 meters) higher and mean global temperatures were about 6-7° C warmer than in 1900.

Only when four Pleistocene glaciations, the last melting about 9,500 years ago, captured and retained much of the world's freshwater in the Antarctic and Greenland polar ice sheets did sea levels attain the levels we have become used to and *apparently* stabilize. That long period (in human, not geological terms) of sea level stability is now over with global climate change driven by human-caused carbon dioxide, nitrogen oxides and methane releases. Simply put, polar ice cover and ice sheets melt when the climate warms, and polar ice is melting faster with every passing year. Another prominent positive feedback mechanism to the loss of arctic ice and the Greenland glaciers is the rapid loss of reflective ice and snow (albedo) from the ocean surface that then causes polar waters to warm even more rapidly. Importantly, we have no verified accurate models to predict the cumulative (i.e. total) impact of these positive feedback mechanisms on climate and water stored in ice on land that will melt and flow to the oceans. In truth, although it is anybody's best guess as to how all of these factors will play out (especially the rate at which these changes will happen), it is absolutely clear that the rate of sea level rise is accelerating every year.

What this translates to for Canada is massive disruption to all existing port facilities, severe coastal erosion in British Colombia, Quebec and the Maritimes, especially Prince Edward Island and Nova Scotia. Nova Scotia is fated to become an island separated from New Brunswick. Much of PEI will be eroded away. Dozens of coastal communities, the access roads and other infrastructure they depend upon will flood in the near future on every marine coastline. Because so many homes, towns and their supporting infrastructure like sewage plants and storm sewers on marine shores were built implicitly assuming that average sea level was constant, almost all of that investment will be flooded, eroded away and lost. Reports of flooding losses will mount inexorably. Coastal Canadian cities, including our key ports of Halifax and Vancouver, will be devastated; others like Quebec City and even Montreal will be stressed seriously.

What is now oceanic flood plain will become shallow seas. Those whose properties are flooded in many of these towns and cities will not be able to retreat to higher ground nearby because that land is occupied already. Private parcels, docks, port facilities, homes, businesses and the infrastructure supporting these investments on shorelines will be submerged. Several million people will be affected directly in Canada alone and the loss of personal wealth now tied up in coastal real estate will be nearly unimaginable. Photographs 1 to 7 show fall, 2011 images of rapidly accelerating coastal erosion in Nova Scotia. Photographs 8 and 9 show the same on the shores of Edisto Island, South Carolina in March of 2011. These images provide just the smallest foreshadowing of what is to come as sea level rise accelerates.

Disruptions to valuable coastal wetlands that support shrimp and larval fish nurseries are inevitable. These wetlands will migrate up-gradient as sea levels rise, but they will not develop into high quality nursery habitat quickly, because flooded structures, toxins stored in soils and infrastructure will interfere with their establishment and growth. Further, the mineral substrates of upland are just not as productive as are long-established organic estuarine sediments. Many decades will be required to accumulate the correct concentrations of organic matter and nutrients to support robust new estuarine wetlands. Large reductions of fishery productivity will follow because coastal estuarine wetlands are the only nurseries for many economically important fish, shrimp and crab species. These losses will cause the collapse of many fisheries that provide seafood protein to a hungry world. One corollary to this damage is that land-based agriculture must then make up large deficits in food supplies, placing more stress on lands and fresh water supplies. This implies huge changes to conventional agriculture and land management as we now practice them. Clearly, when all of these trends are considered, recognized to be interrelated and likely to occur simultaneously, there is no shortage of serious challenges hurtling toward Canadians. The question devolves to this: How do we respond to these inexorable events about to unfold in, and on, "the true north, wild and free.' How we decide to answer this most fundamental question and prepare rationale responses will determine whether the nation prospers, or fails, in the 22nd century.

Another factor contributing to the damage from climate change will be storm events and their inevitable increase in frequency and intensity. Substantially, weather is controlled by oceanic temperatures. Heated moist tropical air masses generally move poleward from southwest to northeast with the Coriolis effect redistributing tropical heat and moisture to the cooler poles. Pacific Ocean currents and temperatures generally dominate Canadian winter and early spring weather and set the continental jet stream patterns year-round. The Atlantic and Gulf of Mexico oceans provide the heat engine for late spring through summer and fall storms, including tropical depressions and hurricanes, in the center and east half of the continent. In essence, it is the warmed tropical ocean waters and their currents that generate the day-to-day weather for North America.

Photograph 1. High tide of September 28, 2011 on Highway 1 at Annapolis Royal, NS. On October 29 and the December 8 high tide touched the tarmac of the paved highway.

Photograph 2. High tide of September 28, 2011 on Highway 1 at Annapolis Royal, NS. During the high tides of late October and December the bottom of this bridge was submerged.

Photograph 3. Savary Park, 15 Km SW of Digby, NS on September 29, 2011. Waves breaking on a rapidly eroding till cliff. A 35 cm higher tide occurred October 29.

Photograph 4. Savary Park, September 29, 2011. Note 20 meter the wide erosion plume moving on the long shore littoral current driven by the wind. Compare to photographs 5 & 6, below.

Photograph 5. Savary Park on November 16, 2011, 48 days after photographs 3 and 4 were taken. Note the collapse of shrubs vegetation along the shore and absence of sand in the gravelly substrate. The till face of this shoreline eroded by roughly 75 cm between these two photos. The sand was moved to the north by the littoral currents shown in photograph 4, leaving only the larger rocks and gravel behind.

Photograph 6. Stairs to the Savary Park beach on November 16, 2011. The till cliff face behind the stairs came to the bottom step in May, 2011 when this new stairs was installed: but, it was eroded about 125 cm back by November 16. Only the top step of this stairway was still supported by the till soil after just six months. Many freshly collapsed trees, shrubs and upland turf pieces were scattered along the shore.

Photograph 7. Rapidly eroding glacial till cliff face on West Mabou Beach, Mabou, NS, August 30, 2011. In the last four years about six meters of this cliff has been eroded.

There is powerful evidence that both the frequency and intensity of storm events has already risen in response to sea temperature increases. Warmer temperatures also mean more water vapor evaporating into the atmosphere from the oceans where much of it will be moved to land. Hurricane Katrina in 2005 and Superstorm Sandy in 2012 may be only the gentlest harbingers of the larger hurricanes of the late 21st and 22nd centuries. Since 1924 there have been 22 catastrophic category 5 hurricanes formed in the Atlantic: but, eight of those have appeared since 2000. And, recognize that it is the historic frequency of intense storm events that engineers and planners have used for decades to guide designs of infrastructure, especially roads, pipelines and storm sewers. The size of the historic 100-year flood event for many localities in North America has increased dramatically in many jurisdictions, especially during the last two decades. The 100-year storm of 1940 has become the 25-year storm in 2013 in many places.

Worse, ocean current patterns are already changing radically. The Gulf Stream of the Atlantic Ocean has for all recorded human history split into a north and south branch and has brought warmth to northern Europe year-round. In the last 3 decades, over 30% of the north branch flow has diverted into the south branch, depriving northern Europe of much of its customary wintertime sustaining warmth. Snow used to be rare in London. Now it happens every year. Great Britain and many parts of coastal Europe are ill-prepared to deal with this reality, having very narrow streets and laneways that preclude effective snow removal and many poorly insulated homes.

Recent winters have shown that Europe is in for a very rough time as climate change accelerates. If the great oceanic global current conveyors that are the engines of temperature redistribution fail or change drastically as many climatologists believe will happen, even more chaotic weather is certain to follow. The effects on Europe will be especially severe. The recent extended flooding in the Canadian Prairie Provinces, heat waves and many other intense unusual weather events are very likely early manifestations of systemic changes to our weather.

Photographs 8 & 9. March, 2011. Beach erosion at Botany Bay on Edisto Island, South Carolina. Thirty years ago an outer barrier island, now gone, was present seaward about 300 meters. The live oaks killed in these photos were several hundred years old.

Ironically, global climate change does not mean that all places will get warmer. Rather, some areas will get much colder as the world's heat redistributing ocean currents change their flow patterns. Eventually, new patterns of weather will emerge as new oceanic currents develop (or fail to develop). All nations, their economies and cultures, have been built on the assumption that weather repeats itself where they live and will be consistent through time: This is no longer true. Agriculture and commerce will suffer great disruptions causing great cumulative and continuous upset to human life styles, economies and cultures in the near future. Some nations that have been the 'haves' will become the 'have-nots'. This will cause enormous political turmoil—especially for nations with rapid population growth.

One thing is certain, as ocean temperatures increase, that heat will spawn more intense weather as the increased thermal energy develops new mechanisms to redistribute the energy captured and stored temporarily in the heated water. What remains to be seen and understood is how, where and when the new weather patterns will develop and exactly what these will mean to human existence worldwide. In a very genuine sense, regardless of where we live, everyone awaits the serious threats of altered weather owing to the man-induced climate change that has already begun.

However, in spite of the inevitable damage to Canada, Canadian losses will be trivial in comparison to the United States, many European nations, parts of west and north Africa, eastern South America, China and India. Some island and low-lying nations (e.g. Bangladesh, Tuvalu [www.**tuvaluislands**.com/**warming**.htm]) will simply cease to exist. Other nations will experience desertification and a nearly complete loss of cropping potential. Many coral atoll island systems, like the leeward Hawaiian Islands, will be submerged. Developed countries like the United States, Holland and Belgium that have much heavy industry and huge home or recreational developments on the existing marine flood plains just above sea level will lose all of this investment. Most east coast and west coast American airports built in these floodplains will be submerged.

Significant parts of dozens of large American cities including much of New York, Philadelphia, Newark, Washington, Charleston, Miami and the bulk of tourist coastal Florida will just disappear. Roughly a third of New Jersey that is home to six million people will be flooded if the sea levels of the Pliocene reappear before recent glaciations trapped up to 27 meters of water in polar areas. A fifth of the present human population of the United States (> 60 million people) could be flooded out and the multi-trillion dollar investments in the infrastructure, homes, industries and recreational areas of the American coastline lost by the middle to end of the 22nd century. One impact will be the destruction of the conventional economic paradigms that most governments of developed countries now aim for—especially the sacrosanct goal of continuous growth.

Canada cannot look to help from other nations to ameliorate or address this impending disaster. We must prepare for this level of coastal impact and continental change in Canada ourselves because virtually everyone else will experience the same serious trouble trying to cope with these inevitable rapid changes, even as human populations continue to grow toward the ultimate density that can be supported. Regional famines and huge population dislocations are inevitable, as is the political and social chaos that will accompany this damage. Another factor that could emerge of very high significance as all of these stressors impact fast growing human populations worldwide is pestilence and epidemic disease. Historically when famine coincides with high population densities of stressed humans, many people die in epidemics. Fortunately, Canada has a relative small population and substantial food resources and is not as likely to experience severe epidemics as many other nations simply because our density is lower. But, Canadians will see these epidemics rampage through other nations.

Just as occurred with Europe after WWI, demagogues will find fertile soil in all this for their pernicious politics. A resource-rich, sparsely-populated Canada could easily find itself dealing with serious civil unrest from within its borders and even larger threats from those that covet our resources and land mass from beyond our borders. Home-grown demagoguery of those offering simplistic or attractive solutions (even if nonsensical) is one likely outcome. This will be a prominent threat to Canadians' freedoms, the Charter of Rights and parliamentary democracy by the end of this century.

In short, the world is headed for a century of ecological, economic and political chaos in the 22nd century as it is forced to deal with the immense impacts of global climate change. A tremendous problem will be climate change refugees inexorably moving inland toward higher ground away from seacoasts, often flooding up against borders of nations with no place to accept them, too few resources to support them and intense domestic resistance to helping alien refugees instead of their citizens. The unsavory political rhetoric that has so dominated the debates about immigration in America from Mexico will become universal complaints in all nations able to accept climate refugees. Whether to accept climate refugees, how many can be accepted and the terms of their presence in Canada will become recurrent topics of Canadian political discourse.

Sadly, our political leadership in Canada continues to bumble forward with platitudes and conventional wisdom, ignoring the serious nature of what is to come, failing utterly to examine the full implications of this situation and provide coherent leadership. Worse, Canada has been ethically bankrupt in its approach to carbon dioxide and methane emissions regulation, especially regarding oil sands developments. The piper grimly awaits his pay; the cost will be very high and the bill will be presented to all of us, regardless of our politics, religion or connections to the powerful elite. The grim reaper will be a very busy fellow as all of this unfolds.

Our current leaders even attempted to deny the reality of global climate change for over a decade (some Canadian Conservatives still do), preferring to harvest the near term political power funded by the largesse of rich and powerful fossil fuel industries instead of leading the way toward a more secure future. The current attitude in Ottawa that these trends are unimportant and can be ignored because we are resource-rich and have lots of time to deal with these problems will condemn Canada to a difficult future. That future could be ameliorated and even exploited for Canadians' benefit, but only if those naïve Pollyanna attitudes that permeate today's politics in Canada, especially among the Conservatives, are changed very soon to address the most probable future.

No amount of partisan rhetoric or denial will change the impending reality. The real physical world does not respond to rhetoric, no matter how optimistic that may be when uttered for near-term solicitation of corporate money and partisan political purposes. An aroused Mother Nature will expend her wrath on ecologies and everyone equally, regardless of political stripe, religion or their responsibility. Who, and which parties, supported policies that lead to these unsavory outcomes will no longer be relevant. Somehow it seems apropos that those whose policies have contributed to these changes will suffer along with everyone else.

5

A vision for a prosperous Canadian future.

I T IS ALL well and good to recognize developing problems, but that means very little without a vision for an alternative future that can address the challenges we face by finding the hidden opportunities. Every crisis has the seeds of opportunity embedded within the impending damage. When rehabilitating landscapes and buildings, ecologists, architects and landscape architects are taught to view every old structure or debilitated parcel of land as both an opportunity and a problem. The problem defines only the challenge to be faced; it is the hidden opportunities that offer valuable solutions. Finding those opportunities typically requires 'out-of-the-box' thinking.

Previously, I have suggested or hinted at certain policies related to immigration and infrastructure that would benefit all of Canada. However, as Canadians we must recognize a crucial constraint we face. To wit, Canada has a weak federal-strong provincial form of government. Compared to the US and many European nations that have strong federal systems with command and control over their states and provinces, the Canadian federal government often has great difficulty coming to agreements on many areas of nationhood with the provinces. In time of crisis, strong federal systems are able to respond more quickly and decisively than weak federal systems that must balance divergent short-term provincial and regional priorities to move forward with a coherent policy for the nation. A second aspect of this weakness relates to accountability: Ultimately, which level of Canadians' government is responsible to address impending change and the problems attendant to it? To whom does the citizen go to get action to address problems? Is it their province or Ottawa? What happens if neither level of government will act, or denies their accountability by blaming the other party (something we have heard all too often)?

Regardless, the Canadian system has endured and works well because of a pervasive culture of accommodation. Canadians will need every bit of that legacy of cooperation and a great deal of patience as we enter the second half of this century—*provided Canadians recognize the immensity of the challenges we face now while there is time to find the opportunities and begin to implement rational solutions.*

Among other prominent constraints is the horrid legacy of mistreatment of First Nations Canadians, both by intention and simple neglect. Canadian governments long ago simply took ownership and control of many native resources ranging from fisheries and wildlife to mineral rights and the land surface by means of poorly kept, often ambiguous, treaties or simple seizure. The legacies of the 'Residential Schools', many unfulfilled promises to improve the infrastructure on aboriginal reserves and many attempts to confine natives on reserves, cajoled there with promises and treaties, or coerced when that cynical strategy failed: that is the sorry and disgraceful Canadian record. It has created a legacy of bitter, disillusioned First Nations peoples that simply have no reason to trust the provincial or federal governments.

The rapid pace of climate change in the north has already begun to stress traditional cultures, particularly those of the Inuit and Denis. Bands like the Cree in Alberta face devastation from the pollution flowing downstream in the Athabasca River owing to the exceptionally disruptive oil sands developments upstream of, or adjacent to, their reserves. However, by no means are these the only unresolved aboriginal issues in Canada, just prominent examples. Rather, every province faces native land claims and unrest of First Nations in conflict with those who now own or control traditional native lands under recognized Canadian law. Importantly, very few First Nations own or control the mineral resources under their reserves. Addressing these unresolved legacy issues will be ever more crucial in the 21st century. These disputes and inequities will not disappear by means of the benign neglect that has been the national policy far too often. The recent troubles at the Attawapiskat First Nation

JAMES P. LUDWIG PH.D

followed by the *Idle No More* protests illustrated graphically the problems First Nations have with unresponsive governments that promise goods and services, but fail to deliver.

As Canadians, we should recognize that the fundamental structure of national and provincial policies toward First Nations has changed very little since we adopted the policies of England that provided the basis for our Canadian code of laws. In doing so, Canada deprived First Nations of many of the rights of land and mineral rights ownership on their reserves that average citizens enjoy and take for granted. As Anglo, French or recent immigrant Canadians we should think about how we would react if our rights to lands were always subject to the threat that mineral rights development would trump our rights to use the resources we were guaranteed by treaty from the surface of our lands. And worse, if extractions of minerals, oil and gas occur, virtually none of the economic benefits would come to us or our people. That is the reality for most First Nations people in Canada. Trouble will continue to bubble up until these gross inequities are addressed.

The North American Free Trade Agreement (NAFTA) and the General Agreement on Tarrifs and Taxation (GATT) have provided considerable stimulus to economic growth in Canada in the last twenty years. However, the preferential treatment accorded the United States in the current NAFTA agreement—especially access to Canadian energy supplies—may not be in the long-term interest of Canada and Canadians. Substantially, Canada ceded a stranglehold on Canadian energy and energy security to the US by accepting NAFTA after allowing infrastructure of the national electrical grid and west to east pipelines to integrate north to south with the US systems.

The most significant consequence of this historic acquiescence is to be hostage to two factors. The first is the (arguably bankrupt) energy policy of the US over which Canada has no meaningful say, let alone any control. The second is the necessity to put up with the negative environmental and cultural consequences stemming from the externalized costs of drilling, mining, upgrading, generating and shipping those fossil fuel products through Canada to the US. The most obvious externalized costs are paid by Albertan's as degraded freshwater quality—especially by the residents of First Nations as part of rampant development of the oil sands. But, there are similar less serious consequences in Alberta, British Columbia and Saskatchewan over conventional oil, gas and hydroelectric energy exports to the US. Saskatchewan, Manitoba and Ontario will have similar impacts from uranium mining that is likely to boom when carbon dioxide controls are finally put in place, elevating nuclear energy to prominence once again.

Under NAFTA and GATT, taxation of these unrefined energy exports to remediate the externalized costs paid by all Canadians, especially aboriginal Canadians and those living near the extractive resource developments, would be very difficult to assess and collect. However, that is a viable pathway toward environmental and cultural remediation of those externalized costs that the US presently avoids completely by importing Canadian oil and gas, often at a large discount to the world price. At this writing, the price differential of Alberta-origin heavy crude oil compared to West Texas Intermediate crude is about $25./barrel which translates to roughly 40 million dollars lost every day or 14.6 billion every year. This is not a 'chicken feed' discount.

Consider this: By 2020, Canada will be exporting upwards of three million barrels of oil and many billions of cubic feet of natural gas every day to the US. Assume export taxes had been levied to compensate Canadians for externalized costs of just 2% of the 2007-2011 average price of these exports (Oil @ $100./barrel; Gas @ $5/MCF in USD). These levies would have produced more than ten billion USD over those five years and more than twice that by 2020. Use of these funds to address the specific environmental and cultural externalized costs of finding, processing and transporting these commodities to the US would be sound public policy. This would redress the externalized damage caused by producing the energy commodities Canada sends south in return for American dollars and accelerated climate change. For Americans, their increased cost would be trivial when spread over the huge volumes they use. For those Canadians contending with the externalized costs on impacted ecologies, communities and cultures—particularly the First Nations cultures—that sum to the health of commonweal of Canada, the benefits would be wholly positive.

Furthermore, Canadians should recognize the unique antiquated way Americans are taxed for their energy consumption. In the US the federal and state governments collect taxes based on the *volume* used. Almost all other jurisdictions tax energy used based on the *price* of the commodity. Americans pay the same basic federal and state taxes on fuels regardless of wholesale price so that there is no increase in cost attributable to taxes when the price of these commodities increase: ***Effectively, the US federal tax rate on liquid fossil fuels decreases with each price increase.*** Thus, there is no gain to the federal government in the US when the base cost of energy commodities increase. This is one reason why American's pay the lowest prices for their fossil fuels of the western hemisphere industrialized nations. In the Americas, only Venezuelans with their nationalized, highly subsidized, oil industry pay less for fossil fuels. In Europe, most fuels cost twice the rate paid in America because European nations tax on value.

Conversely, when fuels like gasoline and diesel increase in base cost in Canada and virtually all other developed nations, their governments at all levels gain more tax and the cost of the energy commodity rises more rapidly than demand alone will support—one important incentive to lessen consumption. Further, as the base prices of energy commodities increase, US businesses essentially gain a competitive advantage over nations that tax on the value of the commodity. American business' competitive advantage grows greater with every increase in commodity cost. Unless this disparity is recognized and addressed in NAFTA, it can only grow larger over time when fossil fuel costs rise inexorably.

Thus, the American counter argument that they already pay energy taxes is flawed and specious in two fundamental ways. Moreover, the argument that domestic US energy taxation policy is independent of NAFTA cannot be sustained. Worse, American energy tax policy distorts the marketplace further with each increase in cost. This alone is justification for a fundamental renegotiation of NAFTA to redress glaring inequities inherent to the two nations' energy policies. If the US is unwilling to renegotiate to correct these inequities, then Canada should simply withdraw from NAFTA. There will be plenty of other customers willing to purchase Canadian fossil fuels and many other raw commodities as supplies dwindle and increase in value inexorably around the world. Since 2012, the price differential has been aggravated by the large disparity in the cost ($15-$30/barrel) of the heavier grades of Canadian Crude compared to the North American standard of WTI. This disparity relates largely to the glut of Canadian oil seeking markets in the US alone and an undersized pipeline system to get it to the single market.

Alternatively, Canada could institute a carbon or consumption tax on all domestic and exported energy commodities under NAFTA that would address the inequities equitably in both nations. But, the present Conservative Canadian government refuses adamantly to consider this rational step towards energy conservation and lowering the rates of North American fossil fuel use. A carbon tax could also help correct the disparity that now controls the price of Canadian heavy crude with relatively more carbon than WTI.

However, for Canada to be truly an independent entity with respect to energy and development decisions in the 21st and 22nd centuries, a fundamental realignment of much of the national infrastructure is required absolutely. Ironically, it is the impending climate change-driven destruction that is opening a window of great opportunity for such incisive actions. As the Arctic warms, the tree line will move north, permafrost will largely disappear well above the Arctic circle and land available for crops will expand greatly in Canada. Existing major ports, particularly Halifax and Vancouver will be devastated by rapid sea level rise, but Hudson's and James Bays will become ice-free year-round to the east and the Northwest Passage will become navigable in all but the coldest months. Geographically, these bays will be at the center of the newly opened lands of the nation and will offer tremendous potential to become the primary ports of Canada, probably near Churchill, MB, Moose Factory, ON and possibly at certain sites in Quebec and Labrador.

Shipping crude oil or refined products from these ports to markets, especially in Europe, would be far easier to accomplish and likely safer than sending either crude oil or refined products to a British Colombia port for export. There is no good reason to focus only on potential Asian markets for Canadian commodities any more than the historic focus on US as a singular market. Canadians should remember that European Brent Crude typically brings a price well above (generally + $12.-15./ barrel) the WTI standard in the US which would be a double bonus to Canadian oil producers and our economy—if only we had the capacity to ship oil to Europe from western Canadian sources.

However, at present, the Canadian north has little developed infrastructure for the transportation of large volumes of goods. Major new developments would be required as east to west connections for the distribution of goods and commodities to and from these new facilities across Canada. Further, major upgrades to the electrical infrastructure and grid of the region will be required regardless of the strategies applied to the placement and designs of other new infrastructure. So, why not address this complex need carefully, with great forethought and wisdom?

Presently, over 90% of Canadians live within 500 kilometers of the US border, forming a thin ribbon of Canadians along the 5,500 kilometer length border with the US. Historically, it was only this thin geographic slice of Canada where Canadian infrastructure was needed. Integration with the US infrastructure systems seemed to be reasonable and far cheaper than building independent Canadian systems when fossil fuels were cheap. A major driver of historic Canadian infrastructure development was the St Lawrence River and Great Lakes with proximity to the industrial heartland of the US and a secure water transportation corridor on which to move commodities and other goods. This will change radically in the 21st century with the weighting of the Canadian population moving inexorably north and westward to take advantage of emerging opportunities.

Resource developments, particularly mining, oil and gas, will be the essential economic engines of this development, underpinned by a more beneficent climate that also supports expanded agricultural ventures. A far more tolerable human existence than has been possible there since confederation will emerge. All of this repositioning of Canadians will create intense demand for a completely new infrastructure including highways, rails, pipelines and an electrical grid to serve the northern region.

A fundamental choice will face Canadians: Do we attempt to protect and hold onto coastal infrastructure and lands as sea level rises inexorably, knowing that strategy is—at the very best—a very expensive short term zero sum game, and in the long term a losing proposition? Or, do we take the impending change we have to respond to as an opportunity to reorient the nation toward intelligent development of the new north and build there for the 22nd century and beyond? What are presently the coastal provinces are sure to face huge economic costs, erosion and flooding losses: That is their future—unfortunate, but true. Developed coastal Nova Scotia, Prince Edward Island, New Brunswick, British

Columbia and the coastal hamlets of Canada's north coast territories will take the brunt of the damage.

When considering these options, Canadians would do well to heed the example of New Orleans and Hurricane Katrina. After that 2005 catastrophe, approximately 114 billion dollars was spent to restore much of New Orleans through 2011. Even with these huge expenditures, significant parts of that city remain devastated. The current US federal final estimate of the total cost is 200 billion USD (www.scragged.com/articles/**katrina**-dreaming). But, all experts agree—'The Big Easy' will be flooded again because the dikes, levees and other flood control measures will not withstand another force three or greater hurricane striking the Mississippi delta region, forcing yet another wall of water up the river and into the city.

Hurricane Sandy (the superstorm of 2012) should awaken all of us to the impending pattern for all ocean coastlines—bigger storms, catastrophic storm surges dealing massive devastation to buildings and infrastructure. The initial estimate of the storm damage in New York and New Jersey was at least 50 billion USD. Interestingly, this was the nearly same estimate provided in the weeks just after Katrina, but the cost to rebuild after Katrina event has already exceeded the initial estimate by more than two-fold and will likely approach four times the cost estimate of 2005. No one ought to be surprised if Sandy's economic effects are as dire.

With hurricane intensities and frequencies rising as oceans warm and rise, the question is not whether, but how soon, will another devastating storm surge overwhelm New Orleans or pounce on yet another vulnerable coastal metropolitan area? Then the people there must ask 'Do we rebuild yet again? If yes, for how many repetitions of the same disaster that will occur ever more frequently as sea levels rise and more intense tropical storms develop? Canada's coastal regions face the same dilemma as sea levels and coastal erosion rates are increasing ever more rapidly (Photographs 1-9).

A far more sensible approach will be to relocate those who are flooded out and to concentrate new infrastructure development where it is safe, remote from climate change damage and geotechnical threats. Canada must build those new port facilities above the elevations that the oceans could reach in order to serve the needs of the entire nation. That is in the north. Geography will dictate that much it will be on the Canadian Shield with its stable geology, a region that most Canadians have paid scant attention to in the past unless they were interested in mining, wilderness recreation or conservation of the taiga and boreal forests ecosystems or rare species.

So, what are the advantages and disadvantages of living and developing facilities in the Canadian north? There are important advantages to *carefully planned development* in northern areas. First, there is a very small resident human population that can be disrupted or might attempt to prevent such developments. With relatively few people to impact negatively, the common anti-development syndrome of 'not in my back yard' (NIMBY) will be a far less common complaint. *However, recognize that many First Nations, their land holdings, treaty rights and cultures will be affected disproportionately. Any building and infrastructure development must credit First Nations rights and be done with their assent in genuine partnerships. Anything less would be another usurpation of their rights and lands.*

Second, the region will be in uncontrollable ecological turmoil as the new climate regime decimates the established sea-ice, boreal forest and taiga ecological communities. In a very real sense, there will be little of traditional 'nature' to save in the north as rising temperatures and altered moisture regimes change virtually everything the long established boreal plant, animal and aboriginal communities have depended upon since the last Pleistocene glacier retreated. Relict existing plant and animal associations will persist on favorable north slopes, but the greater landscape will be changing very rapidly with nothing to ameliorate the pace and direction of those changes. Many new species will invade from the south, and some of these will segue quickly into the dominants. Most of the boreal forests and taiga will succumb to very different invasive ecologies that decisions for wilderness preservation will not address. Many permafrost-dependant communities will just disappear, while discharging their stored methane to the atmosphere, thereby exacerbating the rate of climate change.

Third, the decisions on where and how to build infrastructure can be made far more rationally, with less emphasis on accommodating existing investments or the historic ecologies. Each piece of the new infrastructure can be integrated into a complete system designed to serve the specific modern needs of the population that will come to occupy the north. Finally, because most of the north is underlain by the exceptionally stable Canadian Shield, infrastructure built on this stable geotechnical base will be insulated from tectonic movements and sea level rises that inherently threaten much of the rest of the nation.

The principle disadvantage is the remoteness and lack of suitable bases to support the construction that will be required. The logistics of construction will be difficult, the effort very large, the investments significant and the payback on these slow. There will be very large impacts on First Nations cultures scattered across the north from the sudden appearance of facilities and large numbers of people with their more urban-oriented technical cultures that have never lived in the north, but who will bring the trappings of their life styles with them.

However, the traditional life styles of these local cultures are doomed already by climate change. They simply have no choice but to adapt to this reality if they are to persist in any form. Climate change will be the final insult of a long history of poor and insensitive Canadian federal and provincial government policies toward First Nations. For aboriginals who hope to preserve their traditional lifestyles and cultures, it is a wholly unfair situation. It is yet another case of aboriginal Canadians being hostage to the impacts attendant to being forced to accept a highly developed industrialized culture. Yet, as unfair as this reality is for traditional aboriginal persons, it has the seeds of many opportunities for those able to change and adapt to the new conditions.

The immense opportunity to build the most modern and effective infrastructure in the north should not be underestimated. In the past, most emerging infrastructure decisions took advantage of a relatively local opportunity, most often driven by a single specific infrastructure element, such as developing a railroad line to serve a new territory in the 19th century. Subsequent development then was focused in specific ways and places by the presence of the railroad. For example, when railroads were extended across the nation, towns tended to develop at each major river crossing because rivers offered a water supply for steam locomotives, drinking water for the new population and another cheap means of distribution for goods. Telegraph and telephone then followed. Finally,

JAMES P. LUDWIG PH.D

electrical lines, pipelines, highways, central water treatment and sewage treatment plants completed the skeleton of each local infrastructure system. But, these were built with many conflicts because they were added, really grafted onto, the elements of earlier infrastructure systems already in place, often with little thought of efficiencies. Quite literally, every time a new infrastructure element encounters a preexisting element, conflicts always emerge. Then, the costs to build increase, often dramatically, and uneconomic, even foolish, compromises are made to accommodate growth.

Rarely, was this planned growth in any meaningful sense. It set the stage for fundamental inefficiencies of subsequent infrastructure expansion. Instead, individuals and entrepreneurs were allowed to contribute to development as they saw would benefit themselves the most in the near term, but not necessarily for the commonweal in the long term. In the impending development of the north, a different pattern of infrastructure development could be put in place that addresses old needs and problems and provides far more useable and intelligently designed systems built for the long term.

Examples include the lack of a west to east trans-Canada pipeline and electrical grid system in Canada. These elements could be integrated with a single well-designed east-west infrastructure corridor (EWIC) that incorporates all of the elements needed for Canada to achieve control of its pipelines and electrical energy. If the fundamental infrastructure for the north is built in an EWIC, then the north to south connections to the US become minor means to service the needs of the northern Canadian populace rather than having services to and from the US the reality for Canadians and Canadian businesses. This would be a huge step towards energy independence and would constrain the pervasive influence of the US on Canadian political independence. Then, Canada could export to the rest of the continent only what is in its best economic interest rather than remain hostage to a rapacious neighbor that has shown no signs of losing its appetite for Canada's resources.

It is also interesting to note that if Canada had its own East-West pipeline system in place and did not have to use the existing pipeline capacity that flows a modest amount of western Canadian oil to eastern Canadian refiners through the pipeline system built in the United States, then this existing system that already moves over 2.5 million barrels per day east and south from Alberta is already large enough to accommodate a large increase of exports to the US *without* the very controversial Keystone pipeline. This reality should not be dismissed as politicians on both sides of the border wrestle with how to access and deliver Canadian oil to US consumers. The Keystone is actually needed only because there is no reliable way to move western Canadian oil to eastern Canadian refineries and consumers. Instead, eastern Canadian consumers buy a good deal of crude oil on the world market and pay a huge economic penalty by doing so even as western Canadian oil is sold to the US at huge discounts.

JAMES P. LUDWIG PH.D

6

An East-West Infrastructure Corridor [EWIC] across Canada's North.

PRESENTLY, THERE ARE almost no east to west highways, railroads or electrical lines north of latitude 55-56 degrees north in the central and northwestern provinces, 50 degrees north through Ontario and 51 to 55 degrees north through Quebec and Labrador. What little infrastructure penetration exists in the north, except in the Yukon and western part of the Northwest Territories, is all oriented north to south above this line and built only for local communities. In a very real sense, fundamental modern infrastructure is a nation's skeleton: It is the template on which modern civilization is built. It permits commerce to develop and attracts settlers looking for opportunities. Without that infrastructure, what modern men and women think of as progress and planned development is simply impossible at affordable and competitive cost. Realistically, Canada now has, at the very best, an unarticulated infrastructure skeleton of fragments. It is little wonder that our politicians flounder about, often showing little backbone when dealing with American interests and demands.

It is reasonable to expect climate change to move the distribution of arable land and permafrost in Canada northward between 1,000 and 1,750 kilometers in the 21st century compared to the end of the 20th century, possibly to the edge of the Arctic Ocean eventually. This will open a vast Canadian area—larger than Western Europe—to sustained highly productive development. If Canada wishes to pursue this opportunity intelligently, then an integrated EWIC sited between latitudes 50 and 56 North, extending from roughly Prince Rupert and the Peace River Valley of British Columbia and Alberta to central Labrador can provide huge national benefits in the long term. A 20-40 kilometer wide corridor in which the backbone of an electrical grid, high speed electric rail freight lines, a northern limited access trans-Canada commercial highway system, and pipelines all are planned and sited would give Canada the most secure future that is possible, supported by those essential systems. These would give Canada the most modern infrastructure backbone to support Canada during the chaos of climate change.

Sited deep in the centre of the nation, an EWIC would be more secure from terrorism, far more easily protected than all other options. A suggested potential route could start in the west at Prince Rupert, BC, pass between Ft. St. John and Dawson Creek, then cross Alberta just south of Ft. McMurray, Saskatchewan near Minnissipe, and Manitoba near Thompson. This section of the EWIC would essentially follow the 55th parallel across the western provinces, but then must orient to NW to SE in order to pass James Bay, the southern extension of Hudson Bay, probably between Moose Factory and Fraserdale, Ontario. Then the route could be sited approximately along the 50th parallel past Chibougamau, Quebec before returning to the 55th parallel near Labrador City and then terminating on the eastern shore of Newfoundland & Labrador near Port Hope and Charlottetown, NL.

Small parts of the EWIC could take advantage of existing highway corridors (e.g. highways 16 and 97 in BC; the trans Labrador highway from Labrador City to Happy Valley-Goose Bay, NL). However, about 65% of this route (especially through Manitoba, Ontario, much of Quebec and Labrador) would be through very sparsely settled country in all provinces. Under this scenario, Prince Rupert BC, Churchill, MB, Moosinee/Moose Factory, ON and Port Hope/Charletown, NL become the new seaports for Canada.

An approximate location for the EWIC across Canada's North.

All experts agree, the electric grid in North America is antiquated and exceptionally vulnerable to many threats. The existing grid has collapsed in part on numerous occasions. Essentially, the North American grid is a patchwork system of old elements (many dating to the 1920s and 1930s) held in together by engineers who often have to react quickly to an outage in one place, lest the entire system be tripped out. Its vulnerabilities include the very significant interdependencies across political jurisdictions its immense, ponderous size and a great deal of older, outdated technology. Untoward events in generation stations or failed powerlines in Illinois can precipitate blackouts in many states, Ontario and Quebec at the same moment. Solar storms can disrupt major sections of the above ground grid network, as occurred in Quebec in 1997.

There have been numerous academic studies identifying these vulnerabilities. However, because most electrical utilities are privately owned corporations and user financed, especially in the US, there has been a complete failure to address this situation coherently. The EWIC can address this need for Canada. The potential exists to place major parts of an electrical transmission grid underground to give it significant protection from solar storms and terrorism threats. Further, major sections of such a modern system could be super-cooled superconducting lines that would have negligible power loss over great distances, thereby reducing the transmission losses of electricity substantially.

Owing to the remoteness of the EWIC and the benevolent geotechnical underpinning of the Canadian Shield, nuclear power becomes a real and safe option when built on the shield geology, provided spent fuel reprocessing and radioactive waste burial or containment is sited near the reactors on the shield too. Again, the shield provides the safest and most easily protected place in all of Canada to accomplish these technically difficult and inherently dangerous tasks. Abandoned and played-out mines on the shield may offer technically superior sites for radioactive waste containment and nuclear fuel reprocessing at minimal cost, close to new nuclear facilities, yet remote from dense population centers. These attributes and requirements for the safe use of nuclear power built on the shield as an integral part of the EWIC have the potential to revitalize the entire nuclear industry in Canada and address our greenhouse gas production.

The most pressing transportation needs for the new north will be for the rapid movement of goods for the rest of the country to and from new megaports sited on Hudson and James Bays. There will be a role for both rail and truck transport and both could be fit easily into the 20-40 km wide EWIC with electrified railroads designed and designated to haul most commodities, and trucks many manufactured goods. North to south connections to the EWIC can provide service to the developing northern and existing southern urban and manufacturing centres in Canada.

Each province the EWIC traverses can establish one or more hubs where north-south connections tap the corridor for power, access to commodities and other services. These hubs can be sited where the corridor crosses major rivers, or runs parallel to other water bodies in order to enable the development of domestic and industrial water systems. In some regions it could make sense to build and install a large water distribution system in the EWIC to move waters from regions with large supplies to regions with less fresh water. For example, Alberta and Saskatchewan are very likely to face huge water supply deficits as the Rocky Mountain glaciers melt and fail to maintain the Athabasca, Peace and Bow Rivers at their historic base flows. However, northern Manitoba and Ontario have a surfeit of fresh water that could address this impending water crisis for Alberta and Saskatchewan. Canadians must recognize that fresh water will be increasingly scarce as we go forward and its price/value will reflect supplies and demands, just as any other commodity. A thorough reexamination of the economic value of our fresh water, and our water export and management policies is long overdue.

Provincial hubs also could provide land for industrial parks where new modern businesses and industries can be built. It seems reasonable to suggest that no more than 25% of the length of the EWIC be open to these development zones. Otherwise, the EWIC should be a place of restricted access and carefully controlled developments to preserve this unique Canadian corridor where infrastructure *alone* is maintained in support of the most rapid and efficient cross-Canada transport of commodities and electricity. No competitive nation will have anything like this; high efficiency will be the hallmark leading to sizeable increases in Canadian productivity. The competitive advantage enjoyed by Canadian businesses using the EWIC will be immense and the potential of western gas, oil and mineral deposits fully realized.

Fossil fuels, oil gas and coal will not disappear from modern economies anytime soon. Far too many industries and processes use fossil fuel commodities to produce essential products—oil for plastics and pharmaceuticals, natural gas for nitrogen-based fertilizers, coal burned for industrial power, electricity, chemicals and transportation, etc. Pipelines will continue to be an essential part of the 22nd century economy, even as their importance for distribution of transportation gaseous and liquid fuels moderates. Again, placing all of the commodities moved in pipes within one infrastructure corridor can provide an efficiently serviced means to move these critical materials throughout Canada at the lowest possible cost without reliance on the present US-sited oil and natural gas distribution systems, and electrical grid.

Funding of the EWIC construction elements could include many joint public-private partnerships or crown corporations that are owned by the public. However, ownership of the EWIC lands should remain in the public domain with the use of it governed by the provincial and federal governments and First Nations where their lands are used. For example, the design and construction and maintenance of electric generation plants, the electric grid, rail lines, highways and pipelines can be either private for profit ventures or co-ventures with governments. A reasonable guess of the time and cost to build the EWIC is in the range of one to two decades and 2-3 trillion dollars. Private capital will be required, although a carbon tax on current fossil fuel use or privately purchased minority shares in crown corporations could provide much of the Canadian or provincial governments' contributions and commit the nation to genuine fossil fuel conservation incentives. Moreover, implementing these initiatives could address carbon dioxide emission goals for Canada.

All major projects create controversy and almost always require environmental impact statement (EIS). If one considers this EWIC proposal from the broadest perspective, one factor weighs heavily in favor of it. Virtually every infrastructure element identified above would require extensive environmental review before sited if built one at a time. However, most of these elements have similar environmental impacts. A sensitive river crossing of every element will require most of the same safeguards whether the project element is a pipeline, railroad, highway, electrical transmission line, etc. By placing all infrastructure elements into a single corridor, a single master EIS for the corridor can address virtually all of the impacts of all elements at once. This translates to large cost savings and exceptional efficiencies for the builders, owners and investors. The savings of time alone would be exceptional compared to building each element as a stand-alone entity with its own corridor. However, a master EIS that is comprehensive and protective of the environment cannot be done within the 24 months the current government allows.

Another reason to look at the EWIC is the general principle that 'one man's waste is another's resource.' Consider this example that could be implemented by industries developed close to the EWIC. The Alberta Tar Sands operations produce a significant volume of high quality coke that a steel company could use in their mills. Presently, it is uneconomic to ship this coke to potential buyers because the infrastructure does not exist. Thus, coke and elemental sulfur end up in huge waste piles near the oil sands operations where they are both a disposal problem and a fire hazard. However, a steel company using iron ore from the extensive Baffin Island deposits that built a mill near one of the potential ports on James or Hudson's Bay might contract for all of that tar sands waste coke. The sulfur might find a home in a fertilizer producer that needs it as an additive to their mineral fertilizers. Similarly, a coal-fired power plant built in Saskatchewan, Alberta or British Colombia near the corridor to take advantage of the coal deposits in the west will always use precipitators on their stacks to capture the fine very alkaline flyash, a typical large disposal problem for powerplants. Flyash, owing to its exceptional alkalinity and reserve of reactive calcium oxide, is exceptionally useful to bind salts and heavy metals produced in cutting fluids of oil and gas wells and mineral drilling exploration sites; it can even be used as a Portland cement extender/additive. Thus the powerplant could be a source of a material that by itself is an expensive waste problem, but one needed by the companion industries that will be built on the corridor to treat their own waste streams. These are the kinds of synergies that make an EWIC valuable for all businesses, governments and Canadians, for they will convert problems of the individual business into resources for others, with jobs as a by-product. The commonweal of Canada will be the net beneficiary.

Generally, the best technical expertise for many of the corridor's elements is sustained by, and housed within, the private sector. However, there are exceptions—notably highways and nuclear power plants—where government leadership is either better-suited or essential to success. Regardless, the most difficult political aspect may be how to derive and divide revenues among the public and private investing partners that the use of the EWIC corridor will produce. The rights for private entities to build a given infrastructure element could be auctioned, allowing corporate interests to compete, domestic and foreign individuals or parties to invest, and to generate public funds to maintain the EWIC itself. In this regard, we ought not accept the business mantra that the private sector can always do better than government. Private ownership often means excessive monopoly profits flow back to owners and the public ultimately pays inflated costs for services. Crown corporations, or a variant of those traditional Canadian entities, may offer superior returns to the commonweal—something Americans and capitalists might call 'socialist' as many there describe our medical system.

In essence, corporate interests could participate by purchase of the exclusive rights to build elements of the EWIC. They would recover their investments through fees for transport of commodities carried by their type of infrastructure, the sale of electrical power and a host of other synergies. For example, every electric power plant sited in the EWIC would have to dispose of a great deal of excess heat. By building very large greenhouse complexes next to these plants, even at these high latitudes with short growing seasons, very efficient year-round local fresh food production using the waste heat from electrical generation becomes feasible and realistic. And, transportation of the food produced to urban centres and other markets would be easy, cheap and reliable on the EWIC.

In all provincial and federal jurisdictions there are well-developed means to govern the necessary government-private sector interactions. For example, most utilities and pipelines (whether crown corporations or private businesses) are regulated at both levels of government. There is no good reason to alter these historic relationships; rather, the EWIC will offer many new opportunities to expand and perhaps modernize these cooperative relationships of the public regulators and the private regulated. Prominent reasons to believe these often contentious relationships will benefit from the proposed EWIC include mandates to use the newest technology and materials for all infrastructure elements, a dedicated corridor where the core purpose is the movement of commodities across the nation, and the opportunity to maintain and fine tune these technical operations to the very highest standards of efficiency and safety. Because virtually none of the infrastructure exists now, every element of infrastructure can be built with the most modern materials and technology, very few conflicts between infrastructure types but many synergies.

And, doing these things in a region where there are few people, and therewith far fewer risks to the larger public, is just plain common sense. More often than not, the largest component of infrastructure repair and expansion is owing to infrastructure conflicts and overlapping developments. An integrated EWIC built from scratch can be designed to eliminate almost all of these conflicts. By placing the infrastructure elements within a dedicated corridor where there is no other development allowed except at development nodes where the corridor is accessed and developments are planned carefully, a truly efficient infrastructure skeleton can be created for all of Canada. Importantly, other than investment from US citizens and companies looking to make profits, none of it will be subject to US control. ***Thereby, Canada regains fundamental control of its natural resources—particularly its oil and gas—and its destiny.*** In this writer's view, nothing is more fundamental than this—if our most important civic duty is to preserve Canada as an independent nation.

Policy initiatives of this significance and the investments required of any large project demand intense public scrutiny and debate. As is always the case, the devil will be in the details and there will be many competing interests to weigh in on exactly where it should be sited and built. What would be the most acceptable and effective route for the EWIC across the north? Furthermore, many other ancillary questions of public policy will be a part of the development in the north. For example, is it better to invest billions in fighter jets for the military or upgrade the Navy's capabilities for emerging Arctic operations as the recently-awarded contracts to Canadian ship yards suggest? How do we decide on the best, most equitable and effective means to collect taxes on energy use? Do Canadians confront the existing inane American energy policies head-on, or back away meekly as we have done so often?

Make no mistake, these are monumental issues for Canadians to decide early in the 21ˢᵗ century and *time is of the essence.* How these decisions are taken will determine the success or failure of the nation. Investment priorities and taxation policies are the grist of public policy. These concepts lie at the heart of those issues that will influence the development of the north as global climate change reveals the opportunities to Canadians. We must be ready to grasp them and do so intelligently.

7

A perspective on time and planning.

A S EACH OF us views the world and our place in it, we constantly evaluate our own needs and desires using our values. In reflective moments, we may contemplate our own mortality and what our deaths will mean to our families. Sometimes, especially in moments of crisis or severe threat like WWII, we put aside our aspirations and take great personal risks to assure a viable future for Canada. A central problem with thinking very long term is the absence of a perceived imminent dramatic threat—like war—either to us or Canada. In the absence of real or imagined threats, our tendencies are to expect others to address national problems when we fail to contemplate what is best for Canada.

As politicians have shown us repeatedly, *perceived threats, whether real or imagined, are the surest way to political power.* In the US, linking the 911 attack to the Saddam Hussein regime was used to justify the Iraq war by President Bush. In Canada, Prime Minister Harper set out to build a massive new federal prison infrastructure even as the crimes fell to their lowest rates in 40 years. Both leaders implemented their policies by blatantly dishonest appeals to fear. Changes driven by slow-developing trends are often ignored until they develop into a set of intractable problems that require drastic actions. By frittering away time and placing focus on less important issues, we may squander the chance to act on what is crucial for the long term. Moreover, poorly-justified policies implemented for political reasons or special interests may leave no viable solution or insufficient funds for Canadians to address the genuine problems that are looming.

An analogy to the development of many human cancers is simple, but illuminating. Diffuse non-specific symptoms are noted, but often ignored, by individuals. Often symptoms just seem to come and go for months, but then develop into an acute painful condition that leads finally to a doctor's visit and the diagnosis of an advanced spreading cancer that will be fatal soon. Had this victim acted when the first symptoms appeared, the malignancy could have been treated successfully, but now it is far too late and a premature death looms.

If we consider the trends and changes we now see in our environment signaling climate change, the national infrastructure deficits and numerous cultural issues, then add in the serious states of the economies of North American nations, all the symptoms of massive changes we cannot control and may destroy our freedom unless we act now, are developing in Canada. The only genuine question is whether we, as individuals, and our Canadian politicians, will have the courage and foresight to act now before these symptoms develop into social and economic malignancies that will destroy Canada.

The persistent inattention of governments to these problems is understandable, but not forgivable. Politicians are always preoccupied with getting reelected. Hard choices are almost always avoided in their compelling preoccupation to continue in power as long as possible. Reelection is seldom easy for those who focus on the long term. Yet, this is the perfect prescription for disasters that could be avoided by democracies. Similarly, businesses, especially large corporations with shareholders, are inevitably focused on the next quarter's profits first, with longer term planning relegated to a much lower priority. Sometimes even product development suffers from the preoccupation with profits for the next quarter. These near-term foci often propel the most productive businesses and governmental organizations to a narrow view of the future that sows the seeds of failure in the rich soil of procrastination. For politicians, this strategy works only so long as the public remains ignorant and indifferent to the genuine risks. Remember Abraham Lincoln's famous comment *'You can fool all of the people some of the time, some of the people all of the time, but you cannot fool all of the people all of the time.'* Then, ask yourself 'How have you been fooled by your political leaders? Have they addressed the long-term future of Canada coherently, especially the issues around climate change?' Regrettably, the answers to both questions are no.

Similarly, the necessity to earn a living and feed the family tends to direct the individual's focus only to the short term. Long term needs, especially those related to long term sustainability, tend to be relegated by everyone at all levels of society to a fuzzy future when others, yet to be conceived and born, or our feckless political leaders are expected to solve the problems our generation has ignored or left unaddressed. In times of rapid growth and abundant resources as the world experienced throughout the 20th century, these types of near-term thinking were still viable, even if terribly wasteful. Sustained economic growth and expansion could make up for and correct bad decisions or the absence of a coherent vision of the future.

Unfortunately, that time of benign ignorance and procrastination is disappearing very rapidly because the trends discussed in the previous chapters will coalesce soon into an incredibly challenging future at a moment when worldwide real economic growth may well approach zero or even become negative. Very soon there will be no opportunity to defer the hard decisions to others of future generations. If there was ever a moment in human history when 'time is of the essence' to revise the common short-term pattern of dealing with issues and problems to a long-term perspective, this is it. The luxury of depending on an ever-increasing economic increase is nearly over.

I would posit that the correct length of time for each Canadian to think about Canada's future is a century, well beyond the average lifetime of the individual and about four human generations long. If Canadians adopt this interval of forward thinking and choose those policies that support it, then the nation is assured of a viable future. If not, then Canada will very likely fail to persist, descending into chaos at some point toward the beginning of the 22nd century. Or, Canadians may awaken only to find that Canada was forced into a marriage of convenience with a decadent, poorly governed and militaristic United States where divorce is not an option.

It is worthwhile to consider some scenarios as examples of various ways to plan for the future of Canada. For example, suppose a conventional oil company confronts the need to replace its refinery. Where does that company put that very complex installation? Around the world, most existing and planned refineries are at, or very near, sea level to take advantage of cheap sea-borne shipping of crude oil to, and refined products from, the refinery. Ocean water also offers a cheap wastewater and cooling (heat disposal) strategy: NIMBY is almost always easier to deal with on the ocean shore. Neither fish nor lobsters vote for their interests, and fishermen are merely a minor annoyance for big oil companies unless they have a massive spill, *ala* British Petroleum in the Gulf of Mexico.

However, with an impending eventual 10 to 27 meter sea level rise, tsunami threats and increasing storm frequencies and intensities, will refinery sites and all of the complex infrastructure they require at sea level today be viable in 22nd century? That is not very likely. If one thinks a century out, it would be far better to build the proposed oil refinery where the threats contained in the emerging trends cannot affect the facility even if this decision depresses near term profits. The profits will be recovered doubly in the future if the planning is done well because competitors that failed to plan for the impending sea level rise will be flooded out.

Now, apply that pattern of thinking to all infrastructure elements—power plants, rails, highways, pipelines, etc.—and a whole new way of development emerges for the Canadian future, especially in the emerging Canadian north. Difficult industrial and infrastructure elements are placed in (or relegated to) safe locations only, regardless of the near term cost. Then, the future Canadians not yet born do not have to correct our bad decisions at immense cost and wastefulness. Does this mean that the company building the refinery or developing any facility under this mode of planning will probably pay more to build it in a safe place and possibly to operate the facility for the first few decades of its operating life? Very likely, the answer is yes. Will that deferred profitability be recovered in the future when the safe site continues to be viable and competitors worldwide are seeing their refineries damaged or destroyed? Absolutely! Thus, for this hypothetical oil company, the essential task reduces to convincing their stockholders that the long-term solution is best and the government must insist on it.

To plan and build for a future that anticipates the effects and potential damage that poor decisions today will inflict on the future of Canada, thereby avoiding these threats, this is the greatest obligation of every generation and ethical business. This is what we must train the Canadian populace to do regardless of the near term costs. Psychologists call this 'delayed gratification', something few individuals, corporations and almost no politicians are good at doing. This is what we must demand of our business leaders and politicians and evict those from boardrooms or elected office if they refuse to embrace this principle. Politicians and corporate leaders that are seen to be simply 'in the game' for the sake of power and near term profits, refusing to take the long view, must be ousted from boardrooms and office. Canadians and Canada deserve better!

Such changes to our usual means of thinking will require clear-headed government regulation and considered changes of business and individual thinking at all levels. An early step towards this was the development of environment impact statements (EIS) and various environmental policy acts in both the US and Canada in the 1970s. The EIS process was developed to assure that significant proposed public and private projects were required to consider the effects of their proposed actions largely on the local communities where these were to be sited. Build a mine, paper mill, pipeline or power plant on a waterway and the proponents must disclose the impacts to water quality, vegetation, rare and endangered species, possible reclamation options, etc. for the projected life of the facility. The typical EIS has been focused on the life cycle effects of the proposed facility only on the local area or region, but was almost always limited just to the time of construction and operation of the proposed project. Neither the far future or the nation as a whole were considered by most EIS studies.

A major intent of the EIS process has been to avoid the 'not in my back yard' (NIMBY) syndrome and to do so in a way that maintains the proposed action profitable for the proposer in the short to mid-term. Fast recovery of the investment and near-term profitability are always priorities. How these proposals may influence larger concerns such as the effects on infrastructure and the implications of very long-term effects are considered only rarely (One exception is the consideration given to radioactive wastes from nuclear facilities.). Employment, profitability, and the improved tax-base are always discussed as benefits, although post-project local economic effects after project completion, site reclamation or unplanned shut-downs are usually ignored.

JAMES P. LUDWIG PH.D

These ways of using the EIS process really translate to a large advantage to the proposing entity, especially in difficult economic times or locales where there is chronic underemployment. However, they focus on the effects over the span of one to two human generations only, almost never longer—*because most of the governments that regulate project 'go-no-go' decisions have no policies in place that contemplate the far future and fail to offer any guidance for such vision.* Future EIS practices should be changed to mandate the longest-term view of the impacts of proposed action that is possible. If Canadian federal and provincial governments can achieve this, then we have a bright future. If not, then the long-term prospects for Canada are guarded at best.

It is interesting that the current Canadian government passed legislation that has altered the entire EIS process by forcing all environmental review and decisions into a two-year time frame regardless of the size, scope, location and potential impacts of a proposal. As one who has authored EIS documents for corporate clients, I can attest that this is a most dangerous change to the law of Canada. Comprehensive studies of impacts, especially for very large and ecologically significant projects, often require multiple years of careful field work and analysis that cannot be rushed or compromised without great risk to the commonweal. This is especially true for projects proposed in regions that have no infrastructure and a small human population to support the work required. Clearly, the current federal Canadian government is grossly deficient in environmental expertise and has no sympathy whatsoever for environmental stewardship. Canada's future has been placed in jeopardy.

8

An environmentalist's perspective.

IN MY CAREER as a professional consulting ecologist I have worked for many government agencies, some of America's and Canada's largest corporations and am still a committed environmental activist. In fact, I served as president of the Michigan Audubon Society (Michigan's second largest environmental organization with more than 10,000 members) for two years and was an elected director for ten years. Regardless of these experiences, I am not at all anti-development and have supported well-done industrial and restoration projects of many types. Often, I have disagreed with environmentalist colleagues and occasionally regulators on the merits of proposed development projects. I support all forms of restoration, reuse and recycling as well as means to reduce individual needs.

However, in a world with a rapidly expanding human population it is simply not possible to support all human needs by recycling and reuse. For me the question is more often not whether a project should proceed, but where, when and how it should be done to lessen negative impacts to the greatest degree possible. I also have no objection to corporations making money, so long as it is done ethically and in an ecologically-sound manner. All of us should remember the root meaning of 'eco', that came from the Greek, and means 'home'. Both *eco*logy and *eco*nomics share the same root concept—to develop, protect and sustain the home. The methods and weightings given to the methods of each discipline, and their emphases are very different. But, the core goal of both 'eco' disciplines to protect and sustain home is identical.

For some projects, the questions about what sites are suitable are largely moot. Harbors have to be built where the shoreline and approaches are favorable to safe navigation. Mines, oil and gas wells occur and must be developed where natural forces created an orebody or fossil fuel deposit, not where we might like to have them sited. Further, mined ores can be upgraded to metal concentrates only by the chemistry suited for a particular mineral. Other projects like infrastructure corridors, electrical power plants and refineries usually have much greater flexibility as to where sited. For these kinds of projects, NIMBY and concerns about site suitability are far more relevant. Even so, the devil always lives in the details about any proposed development action. A mine that employs potentially harmful mineral flotation reagents, processes reactive sulfides in water that can lead to acid formation, or one that proposes to use cyanide-based processes has a very different risk profile compared to a taconite iron mine that uses magnets to concentrate iron from chemically benign crushed ores with alkaline host rock. As always, the devil lives in the details of every proposed new facility.

Regardless of the chemistries of the proposed action and processes, all mines, oil and gas well sites should be scrutinized carefully because modern sensibilities require that such sites be reclaimed to new beneficial uses. From personal experience reclaiming mined sites I can attest that ecologically-sound mine reclamation is a tricky matter to recreate a useful landscape where a mine was operated and devastation once dominated the landscape. Conversely, good mine reclamation is almost always feasible. It is the rare mine that cannot be developed and operated in an environmentally sound manner, provided the owners have the commitment and financing to use the best available mining and restoration technology, and their regulators demand it.

Unfortunately, past human actions have left large legacy industrial and mined sites of high contamination. Virtually every marine coastline in North American had industries, utilities and municipalities that left grossly polluted lands in their wake. Many of these sites are going to flood in this and the 22nd centuries. This will bring some of these legacy toxicants into the biosphere where they will cause serious damage, particularly to fisheries composed of species that must reproduce in estuarine wetlands. Realistically, relatively few of these legacy sites can be cleaned up in time to prevent this from happening because the original polluters are either out of business or protected by the 'corporate veil'. Moreover, governments are typically unwilling to prosecute powerful corporations that own contaminated legacy sites if those entities provide jobs now.

However, as proposals for new projects are vetted through the EIS and regulatory processes, any existing legacy sites owned by those companies that propose new developments should have their new project permits conditioned upon clean-ups of their contaminated sites. In essence, regulators must be committed to a policy that those who propose potentially harmful projects must prove their processes are either benign or fully controlled, and that their old projects with legacy pollution cannot be ignored under the promise of new jobs. The corporate 'trick' of bankruptcy to avoid clean-up of legacy sites should never be a valid excuse for regulators to grant permits for new projects by the same management group. In my experience, corporate managers will almost invariably choose the same strategy to externalize pollution control costs to the environment for new projects if it made them money previously, regardless of the ecological risks or damage caused to human or wildlife health. Currently, we often ban white-collar criminals from service on new corporate boards. We should extend that principle to persons who have sanctioned pollution in the past.

This defines a large role for the environmentally conscious citizen. It is human nature for businesses and governments to take the easiest path offered and to make the greatest profit margin possible from their developments. In business, it has often been their choice to externalize costs to the environment through pollution that contributed to their immense profits. In essence, the pattern has been to externalize as many of the costs of pollution control to the environment as the government will allow. Doing what is right to conserve the resource and protect the environment was often relegated to the very last priority, done only when regulators insisted.

Governments have a very spotty record of environmental protection and require the closest scrutiny. In my experience, regulatory agencies operate not to protect the environment first under the law, but rather to protect their employees and power base first; only then will regulatory agencies proceed with their assigned mission. How effective regulators are in their mission often depends on how comfortable the enforcement personnel are inside their agency, not whether there is avoidable pollution in the proposed processes they are tasked to regulate.

Securing their own regulatory power has been the over-riding mantra for agencies for years. This aspect of human nature often leads to inconsistent regulation, even to the point of ignoring laws and regulations the regulatory agencies are charged to enforce. Moreover, in the last four decades there has been a profound shift toward deregulation of corporations and industries of all kinds in the developed world coinciding with the capture of many agencies by the corporations they are supposed to regulate (Gilbertson and Waterston 2008; Chopra 2009; Alexander 2010). Make no mistake, just because an agency has the word 'environmental' in their name is no guarantee that agency will do its job. The people of Walkerton, Ontario learned that lesson in the worst way possible—seven avoidable deaths and hundreds sickened—under the Mike Harris led Conservatives that chose not to regulate municipal drinking water quality stringently in Ontario through budget cuts.

Governments and politicians are terrified first and foremost by bad press and operate on the assumption that the worst thing that may happen is to have bad news released when they are in office, regardless of whether or not they were responsible. 'Spin doctors' have been a part of governments since civilizations developed on the Fertile Crescent and in Egypt over five millennia ago. It is foolish to expect this fundamental aspect of human behavior to change for none of us like to admit our errors. Persons operating out of blind loyalty to their organization, corruptly or without moral intent will always seek to hide the truth or disguise it with rhetoric. The only solution is an informed and engaged Canadian citizenry that ferrets out the truth with an independent fifth estate, then exposes it and discusses the impacts openly in a free society. That defines the primary duty of good environmental stewardship for the citizen: Find the truth about how policies actually succeed or fail, expose it, discuss it and then participate with government agencies to make intelligent policy that protects the commonweal. This is a slow and often cumbersome process, but it does work; and, it protects the commonweal.

9

A new role for the Canadian Military Forces.

OUR CANADIAN FORCES have a distinguished record of service and accomplishment in the 20th century, both in war and peacekeeping. Ever since Canadian loyalists assembled militias to protect Upper Canada from American invasions in the war of 1812, the Canadian Forces have performed heroic feats to protect Canada and the British Commonwealth. Many soldiers and their families sacrificed lives to address tyrants abroad in foreign wars. That acknowledged, there are realities to Canada's military situation that should be faced, and new roles for the military that can benefit the nation domestically. It is long overdue to reconsider the role of the Canadian Forces.

The first reality is that Canada is insulated from potential Asian and European aggression by oceans and the Arctic where the logistics required of any aggression towards Canada would be immense, very complex and wholly detrimental to any military incursion. This is not true for our southern border with the United States. If Canada is to face any real military threat in the 21st or 22nd centuries, the direction will be from the south and the United States. America's goal will be the acquisition and control of Canada's resources. In any hypothetical confrontation, the military advantages of the US are insurmountable: with 90% of the Canadian population living within 500 kilometers of the unmilitarized border, short logistic supply lines and a vastly superior American military in both manpower and equipment, an aggressive America would win every war.

Moreover, much of the defensive capability that exists in the Canadian Forces lies in arms purchased from US corporations; parts and services for that equipment would not be available in any hypothetical conflict. Bravery and resistance of Canadians would not carry the day for Canada. The only protection that Canada could expect would come through the good will of other nations and sanctions they might apply to the US in support of Canada. But, international good will does not win military battles and control of important resources becomes the law following an invasion just as the Iraqis have learned about their oil reserves since the Saddam regime was toppled there. It is no accident that American-owned and controlled oil companies now control Iraq's oil through concessions acquired after the war.

The second reality relates to the effectiveness of Canadian participation in foreign wars, police actions and similar efforts. Canadians should draw a distinct line between peacekeeping or humanitarian missions and those that involve military force for a military goal. Specifically, we should not let Canadian Forces be part of an American led global police force, especially when the goals of military actions relate more to the US securing access to energy and material resources than to humanitarian efforts. Canada should be very careful not to participate in efforts to kill terrorists in other nations at the behest of the US. Many commentators have noted that killing terrorists overseas is an open invitation for allies of those same terrorists to export their violence to Canada. Participating in these misguided American led efforts can only promote more worldwide violence, particularly in, and from, fundamentalist Muslim nations. Worse, such actions only serve to justify those who believe in promotion of the 'fortress North America' concept. The ancient aphorism 'Let sleeping dogs lie.' applies here.

The third reality for the Canadian Forces is that they are the best-equipped and led part of Canadian society to approach the development of the Canadian north effectively. A very large part of development of the Canadian north will relate to our need to fortify, protect and occupy our Arctic lands and waters. In this regard, the recently announced 33 billion dollar procurement project to replace the aging fleet with vessels built mostly for Arctic patrol and life-saving missions is an excellent first step towards reinforcing Canadian claims to Arctic lands and resources on the seabed at the internationally-recognized territorial limits. Canada must be able to project both policing authority and life-saving capabilities in the Arctic to be credible on the international stage. For this we need Arctic military bases, logistic capabilities, capable ships and ports. Presently, we have very modest (some would say miniscule) Arctic capabilities compared to either the Americans or Russians.

Conversely, the intent to invest a like sum for a new purchase of F-35 fighter jet aircraft from US suppliers seems utterly wasteful and foolish. This is especially the case because the new Arctic patrol ships will be built in Canada. But, the F-35 aircraft and their maintenance parts will be made mostly in the US. Keeping our investments here where they produce domestic jobs is ever more important, especially since the American Congress requires typically that only American firms are eligible. Another aphorism applies here: 'Sauce for the gander is sauce for the goose'. America should not be allowed to have it both ways, grasping the benefits of free trade, but refusing those in kind to Canada. All Canadians, not just those engaged in forestry and agriculture who have experienced damages of the American approach to NAFTA, should recognize that this one-way slant has been the pattern of American commerce under NAFTA for nearly two decades. Ultimately, acquiescence to this reality damages all Canadians.

So, assuming that the international roles for our military should be changed, even as we pay close attention to the economics and utility of military procurements, what is a better role for our Canadian Forces on the 21st century? My answer is simple: Use the proven engineering, logistic and leadership talents of the Canadian Forces to spearhead the development of the East-West infrastructure corridor as well as the new military capabilities in the Arctic. In truth, there is no other Canadian federal agency with the organization and talent existing and able to tackle such a daunting and complex assignment. Moreover, by integrating the two needs for a completely new northern infrastructure and Arctic military bases into a single project, very large operational efficiencies can be achieved.

The Canadian Forces have all of the functional elements required for this assignment including the organizational structure, much of the equipment required, medical and other support staff and a proven history of competent combat engineering. In a very real sense, preparing the north for infrastructure developments will be a lot like combat. Supplies, logistics, organization and a singular focus to deal with the harsh conditions will be the most crucial assignments, just as in battle. These are proven capabilities and strengths of our Canadian Forces.

It also reasonable to evaluate other needs and unfulfilled commitments to the aboriginal communities of the north. We all have seen the heartwarming noble work of the Canadian Forces in Afghanistan over the last decade building schools, installing new water and sewage systems and providing clinics and health care services to remote villages. Over the same period, we have seen precious little of that delivered to Canadian First Nations from any government agency, whether our federal government was under the control of Liberals or Conservatives.

If we accomplish these desperately needed tasks for Afghan villagers half a world away, how can we justify leaving First Nations Canadians in the north with no clean water, inadequate sewage systems, poor medical care, substandard housing etc.? But, that is exactly what we have done, and we must face up to this reality. It is utterly shameful that we have not kept our commitments to the peoples of our First Nations. The Canadian Forces could be reoriented to this address task; that alone would alleviate many negative social influences on First Nations reserves. Our collective failures to address the needs of our own First Nations after two centuries of unconscionable national policies should be a considerable goad to get on with the tasks required.

Assuming the Canadian Forces were given the assignment to prepare the north for infrastructure development and assist First Nations, how could this be paid for? One simple means would be the energy tax on exported oil and gas suggested previously. At the export rate of oil and gas in 2010 and a 2% hypothetical tax, 1.78 billion dollars could have been generated on the oil alone. Assuming the projected rate of 3 million barrels per day of liquid fuels (mostly crude oil) by 2020, a 2% tax and a base price of $100./barrel would generate about four billion dollars annually from oil exports to the US alone. Alternatively, Canada could level a carbon tax on all consumption of energy commodities whether by US or Canadian consumers and that would generate considerably more for these tasks. And, a carbon tax might be easier to implement under NAFTA because it would apply to all users of Canadian-produced fossil fuels, not just those exported to the US.

This amount of funding could go a considerable way towards paying for the work recommended here. Further, if we spend it on Canadian Forces working on assignments in Canada, the money stays here and is recycled (generally six times) benefitting far more than just those getting the new services directly. This is the sort of economic stimulus that can benefit every Canadian. Buying unproven F-35 jets from America is not.

Another consideration is domestic jobs. The military has a long history of giving direction and the first real jobs to unfocused young Canadians. With unemployment hovering between 7 and 8%, placing the focus on the Canadian North and using the Forces there could help address the employment deficits of the nation in a very socially beneficial way. This could even help address the chronic underemployment pattern so many talented and well-trained immigrants to Canada face. Many immigrants have found that their advanced degrees earned overseas mean very little here in Canada where they face cumbersome professional certification bodies. We do not need competent foreign-trained engineers and doctors driving cabs in Winnipeg and Toronto. We could use a military-based program as a means to offer these kinds of exceptionally valuable immigrants an opportunity to use their skills precisely where Canada needs their help. In return, this program could give these new Canadians ample opportunities to prove their skills, professional competence and expertise in a properly supervised and evaluated context. This system would help them move into the mainstream of their professions far more quickly in Canada than occurs presently.

As Canadians, we should consider the history of two Great Depression programs that America used to great benefit. The New Deal of President Franklin D. Roosevelt instituted many programs to employ the unemployed, ranging from the Civilian Conservation Corps to the Works Progress Administration. These programs gave millions of the unemployed people meaningful work to do and addressed many of the infrastructure deficits of America including roads, national forests development and four huge hydroelectric dam construction projects that have provided about 8% of the electric power used in America for seven decades. The benefits of those investments helped win WWII and have continued to benefit

America ever since. The second American effort worth considering as a model is the US Army Corps of Engineers, a branch of the US military that has addressed certain US domestic infrastructure needs for over a century, especially those associated with dams and maintenance of navigable waters.

These are example American programs that Canada would be wise to emulate through a fundamental reorientation of the Canadian Forces to our domestic needs. Mr. Roosevelt got it right in 1933 and so should Canada in the 21st century. Leave the wars to the Americans if they want to continue to be so foolish as to expend their precious resources and the lives of their people in foreign lands for whatever dark or foreign policy purposes they may wish to pursue. We can do better than that for Canadians and our heroic Canadian Forces by assigning them honorable Canadian tasks for the benefit of all Canadians right here at home.

10

Perspectives on myths about taxation and health care.

MY FAMILY BACKGROUND includes unshakable commitments to higher education, science and public service. A brother, uncle and father all were American physicians in general practice and surgery. They served in the American military from WWII through the second Gulf War. They practiced medicine during the privatization of US health care and the emergence of the hybrid US government-paid for and private health insurance system in America. My brother and father warned me to expect poorer health care before I moved to Canada and to expect to pay far more income taxes. Furthermore, an American colleague in science shared the same concerns. Before accepting a Canadian Research Chair position he conducted a thorough analysis of the two tax systems in 2004.

Our experiences have proven the myths about Canadian taxes and health care to be wrong. My friend's analysis revealed a 1% higher total Canadian tax burden above the total US tax burden in 2003. Today the total taxation rates are virtually identical, but collected by different entities with provinces taxing more than states, but the Canadian federal share being proportionally less than the US federal share. Much of the total Canadian tax burden comes through value added taxes at the point of purchase (HST and GST [sales taxes]). Conversely, in America sales taxes are left exclusively to the states.

My own experience verifies this analysis. In fact, my total tax burden actually fell by roughly 3% after 2000 compared to what I would have paid had I continued to live in Michigan. In my experience, it is a pernicious myth that Canadians are taxed more than Americans. Individual Canadians are taxed in different ways, but not appreciably more than Americans. Similarly, corporate tax rates are similar between the two nations with the US stated rate greater than in Canada. However, in the US there are far more subsidies and 'loopholes' for corporations to use to avoid taxes so the effective tax rate (i.e. what is actually paid) in the US is very close to Canada, notwithstanding the feverish rhetoric from Republicans to the contrary.

Moreover, hidden within these numbers is a stark reality for Americans. Canadian universal health care is a governmental responsibility, paid for by federal and provincial taxes. Health care for Americans is provided through a very selective (some would say inequitable) massive system of private health insurers and hospitals. Individuals obtain coverage by insurance provided by employers or themselves. There are deductibles and limitations on coverage that vary widely depending on one's ability to pay premiums. There is a strong incentive for American companies to provide the absolute minimum of health care coverage for employees.

Millions of Americans were ineligible for even the most basic coverage until recently and there were widespread protests from the political right against recent extensions of coverage (popularly referred to as 'ObamaCare') to include most, but not all, of the working poor. Presently, the American Federal government pays only about 41% of health care costs, the remainder coming from private insurance policies paid for by individuals or their employers. The American political debates over how to control these costs are vitriolic and pit the well insured employed against the unemployed and uninsured poor. The American health care system is now a microcosm of class warfare.

Comprehensive health insurance coverage for American families is incredibly expensive, now averaging $1,584./ month for a family. $8,088. USD *per capita* was spent in 2009 in the US, compared to $5,614. Cdn in Canada in 2010. In 2009 the US spent 17.6% of the total gross domestic product on health care compared to 11% of GDP in Canada in 2010. Thus, the American health care system costs more than 60% more than the Canadian system (CHCH, 2011; CIHI, 2011).

Private insurers and most American hospitals are for profit entities. The snowstorm of paperwork that accompanies private coverage and reimbursements from the government and insurance companies is daunting, slow and costly. There are numerous places for fraud to grow luxuriantly in the American health care system. An immense cadre of inspectors and administrators in the private sector and government are employed to deal with this cumbersome system. These 'paper work' health care personnel deliver no health care—that is done by the doctors and nurses funded through the system. But, they and the profits of private insurers, sop up a huge part of US health care funding. President Obama and the democrats have studied this carefully and found 716 billion dollars per year expended to 'middlemen' in the Medicare part of American health care alone.

From a cost perspective, 17.6% of the US Gross National Product budget went to support health care in 2009 and those costs have been rising on average 6.8% per year since 1999. Some have projected that American's health care could grow to 25% or more of GDP as the 'baby-boom' population ages. As a small businessman operating in Michigan from 1977-1994, paying premiums for healthcare of my family and employees began at 7.1% of salaries in 1977 and grew to 11.6% of salaries paid by 1994 when I closed the US offices and moved all operations to Canada. In Canada, the only health care related costs I have relate to seniors prescriptions and term insurance to purchase health care coverage when I am out of the country on business or vacation. I spend less than $600. for all my health care as a seventy-two year old Canadian retiree annually.

Moreover, the efficacy of two health care systems is measured most accurately by the satisfaction of those who get the care and the mean life span of those living under each system. In these metrics, the US health care system fails compared to our Canadian system. Canadians are consistently more satisfied and proud of their universal Canadian health care system than Americans. Canadians live longer lives by about 2.9 years on average than Americans, in spite of fact that the *per capita* cost of the US system far outstrips the Canadian system. The following comments from Wikipedia seem to sum up the difficulties and deficiencies of the American system accurately:

"For everyone else, health insurance must be paid for privately. Some 59% of U.S. residents have access to health care insurance through employers, although this figure is decreasing, and coverages as well as workers' expected contributions vary widely.[25] Those whose employers do not offer health insurance, as well as those who are self-employed or unemployed, must purchase it on their own. Nearly 27 million of the 45 million uninsured U.S. residents worked at least part-time in 2007, and more than a third were in households that earned $50,000 or more per year.[25]

Despite the greater role of private business in the U.S., federal and state agencies are increasingly involved in U.S. health care spending, paying about 45% of the $2.2 trillion the nation spent on medical care in 2004.[26] The U.S. government spends more on health care than on Social Security and national defense combined, according to the Brookings Institution.[27]" [Wikipedia]

Individually, I believe I have had superior health care since moving to Canada. The Canadian physicians I have had as family doctors and specialists have been focused on preventative medicine first, and have never rationed care. My worst complaint is that sometimes it takes longer to see a specialist than I would prefer. To be sure, there are problems with the Canadian health care system including uneven distribution of doctors and nurses across the nation, wait times and a generally longer time to acquire funding for new specialized medical technologies than in the US, but many rural areas of the US have the same problems. However, for the vast majority of Canadians, the health care provided is far better than just adequate. In my experience, it has been superior without longer wait times or poorer access than I experienced when living in the US.

As a Canadian citizen and resident, I take for granted that universal health care is my right, and pay no attention whatsoever to budgeting for health care issues. I sleep far better than many Americans, absolutely secure in knowing that basic universal health care will be there for myself and my family. I can move anywhere in Canada, take any job I chose, move to another job if I wish and health care is always there, no questions asked. Health care is not concern of my workplace and has no influence in the choices I make about who, or what entities, I chose to work for.

Hidden within these large differences in healthcare is an important economic and social reality for all Americans. In the US, every individual and business must confront health care costs as a very large piece of their budgets and cost structure. Worse, medical care coverage is only provided when someone pays the premiums to the private insurers or by emergency rooms of public hospitals where wait times are always long and the efficacy of treatments is lower. Most private insurance policies limit coverage for catastrophic illnesses severely, leaving many individuals and families at risk of bankruptcy if they are unlucky enough to experience a catastrophic illness. It is of considerable interest that the mandates of ObamaCare that drew so much Republican fire in the recent presidential election included the requirement that insurers could no longer ration health care based on pre-existing medical conditions. Quite obviously, having to cover preexisting conditions will reduce private insurers' profits.

When one loses or leaves a job that provided insured coverage in the US, the money must be found to buy new coverage; that takes money away from other needs and opportunities. Moreover, this reality can be a strong incentive to keep on doing a demeaning or overly demanding job, since coverage from a different employer often comes with severe limitations on what preexisting conditions are covered at the moment the new policy starts. Insurers in the US are in business for profit first; service to their insured parties comes second. Insurance company administrators are very often the *de facto* 'gate-keepers' to US health care, but doctors are in Canada.

While health care costs in the US are not a tax *per se*, they function exactly as though they were a tax in terms of budgets. Health care insurance and deductibles reduce the disposable income of the individual and decrease the productivity and competitiveness of US businesses. It is no accident that health care costs for employees and retirees of companies have become a prominent part of every major labor negotiation in the last two decades in the US. Companies seek every means possible to lessen their contributions to health care plans. Some American corporations, perhaps most notably General Motors, even resorted to bankruptcy to control their health care costs. Others have used health care as an excuse to outsource jobs and investments to third world nations where there are few or no mandated health care standards and negligible costs.

When one looks carefully at the two nations' health care systems, the cumbersome inefficiencies of the American privatized system should be regarded as a serious drag on American economic growth. The US is presently the only developed nation in the world with a private-for profit health care model; all others have some form of universal health care—even Mexico. And for every other nation the OCED has studied, health care costs as a percentage of GDP are much lower than the US pays, Japan paying about 8% of GDP and even Great Britain just 8.9% of GDP. In terms of health care cost, America is in a league of its own.

One result of the universal Canadian health care system is that many North American businesses regard this as a compelling rationale to invest in Canadian manufacturing facilities for two salient reasons: the governments bear these costs, and our work force is likely to be more healthy than a US labor pool simply because Canadians live longer than Americans and overall enjoy better health outcomes. From the Canadian side of the border, as a dual citizen I cannot understand the rationale of many US politicians. It should be obvious to anyone with a brain that government-paid (single payer) universal health care would be an enormous stimulation to the whole US manufacturing and services sectors and would save everyone (except the private insurers and doctors) boatloads of money. This is where Americans should look for a true economic stimulus program.

11

Cultures and the pernicious neoliberal political landscapes.

A S I WROTE the first draft of this essay in the summer of 2011, I was entertained by two ostensibly Canadian television ads of beer producers touting Canadian values to sell traditional Canadian brands. The first of these for Sleeman Beer touted the checkered history of a company founded by sly pirates that used their 'ill-gotten gains' to open a Canadian brewery that once supplied beer to Al Capone's gang during American prohibition. Similarly, the Molson's Canadian beer ad touted the lands we walk on (the Canadian Shield), the canoes we paddle, our Rocky Mountain vistas and the lakes we recreate on as the base of Canadian values. Viewers were invited to conclude these values are what makes Canadians different compared to crass Americans that presumably make poor choices to drink inferior brews. There was a cheeky Canadian flavour to these ads that were really subtle digs at American values and hubris. After all, Americans make good opponents in hockey, so why not in beer consumption?

However, it is doubly ironic that both beer companies were founded in Canada but are now owned by foreign corporations—Sleemans by Sapporo of Japan, and Molson's Canadian by Coors Brewing of Colorado, USA. Regardless, the beer ad gurus that concocted these commercial messages understand the Canadian psyche well. There is no mention at all of the true ownership of these iconic Canadian brands. The ads are aimed squarely at how we evaluate ourselves against Americans. One may suppose that this is the inevitable way Canadians are induced to think by the mere presence of the massive political and economic machine that is the United States on our lengthy border.

Conversely, I have been offended by an ad prepared by Exxon-Mobil (the world's largest oil company) stating that American energy security is tied to the development of their Kearl project in the oil sands of Canada. The ad invites the American consumer to conclude that American access to (even control of) Canadian oil is a foregone conclusion, that Canadian interests in, or ownership of, the resources have no bearing on the matter of 'North American' oil supplies. In Exxon's view, the location of the Kearl project in Canada is irrelevant so long as it is in North America; Canada has no real say in how the resource is developed and used by Americans. What incredible hubris!

Clearly, Exxon believes it is merely an unfortunate complication that Canadian sand somehow got mixed up with American oil, but this fact of resource location is just a minor annoyance to the world's largest corporation. Moreover, Americans ought not to worry because 'good old Exxon' will fix that tiny complication for American consumers! Perhaps worst of all is the subliminal message that the world's largest corporation knows what is sound American energy policy, when what Exxon-Mobil really does is to make money by the truckload by exploiting the energy resources of many nations from Canada to Iraq, notwithstanding the interests of the American consumer. In 2010, after a "difficult year" Exxon-Mobil reported a *mere profit* of 30.5 billion USD.

It certainly is galling to have much of our Canadian culture and economy so grossly influenced by the presence of this arguably sloppy and insensitive economic giant, replete with many pompous critics of Canadian institutions sprawled on our very doorstep. It is rather like having a fat overbearing relative that inevitably spews lots of fatuous advice over for Thanksgiving dinner, therewith having to endure their presence, unwelcome advice and prattle only because they are family when what you would really like to do is tell them just to shut up so that everyone might simply enjoy a nice dinner.

However, the recent political and economic turmoil in the United States has revealed stark failures and the enduring hubris of the giant, exposed numerous fallacies and weaknesses its republic style of market-driven democracy. Most significant is a fundamental failure of American style market capitalism to provide equity for its citizens. American wealth has been concentrated into multinational corporations and the hands of an elite few, leaving the middle and lower classes to shoulder the tax burdens of the greater American society. To a lesser extent, the same pattern of taxation and wealth accumulation has emerged in Canada too. Henry Giroux put it this way when discussing the negative effects of neoliberalism in the United States (Truthout, April 7, 2010):

> *'For over 30 years, the American public has been reared on a neoliberal dystopian vision that legitimates itself through the largely unchallenged claim that there are no alternatives to a market-driven society, that economic growth should not be constrained by considerations of social costs or moral responsibility and that democracy and capitalism were virtually synonymous. At the heart of this market rationality is an egocentric philosophy and culture of cruelty that sold off public goods and services to the highest bidders in the corporate and private sectors, while simultaneously dismantling those public spheres, social protections and institutions serving the public good. As economic power freed itself from traditional government regulations, a new global financial class reasserted the prerogatives of capital and systemically destroyed those public spheres advocating social equality and an educated citizenry as a condition for a viable democracy. At the same time, economic deregulation merged powerfully with the ideology of individual responsibility, effectively evading any notion of corporate responsibility, while effectively undercutting any sense of corporate accountability to a broader public.'*

As we consider what Canada ought to aspire to become in the 22nd century, it behooves Canadians to consider the cultural, economic and political landscapes of the two nations most carefully. As Canadians, we should learn from the mistakes of America, and come to understand the actual impacts of the flawed American vision, hubris, military might and economic dominance on the future for all nations. We should be wise enough to select what is good of the American way of doing things, and reject what has failed to produce the common good for all Americans and now threatens the greater economic and cultural stability of all nations worldwide.

JAMES P. LUDWIG PH.D

Citizens develop their worldviews from birth and the ways their elders present the world, their nation and obligations of their citizens to their country. Children grow up and mature singing their national anthems; immigrants learn the anthems as a part of their citizenship quest. In America, the story told in the Star Spangled Banner anthem is of a battle for an obscure military fort near Baltimore under siege. Americans repelled a British force successfully that had attacked savagely with 'bombs bursting in air and the rockets red glare' during the war of 1812. But, the American flag was flying over the fort in the morning, saved by brave Americans that fought to secure their freedom. On the surface, it is a wonderful story of exceptional patriotism.

But, all of the images presented by the American national anthem are militaristic, celebrating the freedom secured with violence and brave determination in battle. The music to which the anthem is set is nearly as bombastic and strident as the words. In fact, the tune is actually an old British pub tune, a type of music known neither for its beauty or capacity to be sung easily, as many an unfortunate vocalist at sports events has learned to their considerable chagrin. It has always reminded me of the bombast in Mussorgsky's *Great Gate of Kiev* passage from his *Pictures at an Exhibition*.

Contrast the American anthem to the Canadian National anthem, *O Canada*, that soars much like Beethoven's Pastoral sixth symphony, and celebrates Canada as 'the true north, wild and free', ending with the singer's pledge to protect and nurture the land and its people. Two anthems as different in tone and musicality as night is to day, each replete with hidden messages to their respective citizens! We should remember the Black Panther Eldridge Cleaver's famous line that 'Violence is as American as apple pie.' uttered in the 1960s. Americans did not like it then, but it was true then and remains true today as the Arizona shooting of Representative Gabby Giffords and massacre at Newtown Connecticut have shown us. The American national anthem only strengthens the subliminal message that violence with guns and the wanton exercise of military might are as acceptable to Americans as apple pie. It helps explain how Americans came to be recognized worldwide for their seemingly universal hubris: it is embedded in their psyche by their earliest experiences and socialization. It requires neither thought, nor sound judgment, for Americans to default to military solutions to national problems or the guns in private hands to solve domestic squabbles.

In a similar vein, compare American and Canadian football. The American game is played on a smaller field with far less area to use to score points. Americans have four downs to secure a first down in order to continue possession of the ball and to attack their opponents. Americans tend to play a game dominated by the brute force of the running game. Canadians use a much wider and longer field, particularly in the end zones, have only three downs and rely far more on the elegance of the passing game. Americans allow only one man to be in motion and only movement parallel to the line of scrimmage before the play begins. But, Canadians allow many to move simultaneously and they all can move forward toward the line of scrimmage before the play begins. The American game is basically a brutal ground game closer to rugby. But, Canadian's play a far more elegant—even balletic—game, a celebration of space and speed, suited to a larger nation with a far sparser population that aspires to be 'wild and free'.

During the 2011 Army-Navy game, two football programs of the American military service academies that ranked first and fourth of all 120 American division one universities for their ground game in that season, the two teams ran 94% of the time trying desperately to grind down their opponent by brute force. Was this an accurate reflection of two centuries of the American warriors employing overwhelming military force to achieve their goals? The young men in these iconic American service academies will be the leaders of America's military in two to three decades. It is reasonable to expect them to default to the socialization and values of their militaristic and football cultures when they lead their troops into the battles during the 21st century.

Now, make no mistake. As befits one born and schooled in America for two decades, I am a rabid fan of both nations' versions of the game. I am ecstatic when Michigan beats Ohio State and despondent when they lose to those much reviled (in Ann Arbor) Buckeyes from Columbus. As a high school level player in America over fifty years ago, I loved the game, learned a great deal about my own capabilities, limits and how to succeed through the personal challenges of that violent context. Football demanded teamwork, hard work, pain and sacrifice. However, the differences between the two versions of football is illuminating for these games reflect the soul of the two cultures.

I once took a British immigrant to Canada who knew nothing of the games of North American football to see a University of Michigan game at the famous 'Big House' (the largest college-owned stadium in the world) in Ann Arbor. My colleague was trying to figure out why it was so difficult to understand Americans and negotiate with them as a representative of Canada; Americans simply did not act like the polite and self-effacing Canadians he had dealt with for three decades. Nor did they reflect the British model for respectful relationships under which he had been raised. He could not understand why Americans seemed to act from hidden agendas, often defaulting to brute force, rarely genuine compromise. I suggested that seeing an American football game would help him understand Americans. He was skeptical, but agreed to humor me by attending one. A former Wisconsin all-state high school fullback who shared our academic and ecological interests accompanied us.

As the game unfolded, we Americans explained how the game was structured and pointed out the running plays that depended the brute force of good line play, how the deception and fakes built into plays made accomplishing the goal of scoring points easier and how the aerial game played a role in the outcome. Slowly it dawned on him that football was a very good way to begin to understand American tactics in international relations. Over-run and destroy the enemy by brute force, default to deception to win the victory or fool the opponent with an unexpected pass. Celebrate a good hard-hitting defense or the ignominious defeat of the opponent. Reward the bravery of the home players by the fans' cheers. Watch the university marching band play the American national anthem. See the crowd and team inspired by the University 'Victors' fight song, a rousing piece of martial march music that could serve as a setting for any set of aggressive or inappropriate militaristic words some fool might set to this iconic Michigan anthem. He saw a fundamental aggressive America in an emotionally charged microcosm of its culture—stripped of artifice and control, where attitudes, tactics and even worldviews were exposed graphically, if one just looked and considered carefully.

As he studied the crowd reactions to the Michigan victory that day, America and the fundamental bedrock attitudes and tactics used by

Americans in negotiations finally began to make some sense to him. Canadians should understand and appreciate that Americans are socialized into a military frame of reference from their earliest exposures to the American concept of nationhood, their national anthem and extending even to their most cherished national sport. These subliminal messages and ways of approaching others that they deal with are as ingrained to Americans as their DNA.

Canadians cannot change this pattern of American culture and socialization, although we could show Americans a better way forward by example. But, Canadians must deal with this reality in every aspect of their relationships with Americans, whether in business, cooperation over border issues, decisions about pipelines, etc. For, those are the very bedrock assumptions of American values, what actually drives their worldview and the way Americans see others. Fundamentally, once all the artifice is stripped away, Americans see themselves as the most favored of peoples and nations with *carte blanche* to dominate and conquer others. Whether the game is politics, business, war or football makes no difference; this is the American Way.

The American Way and a market-driven economy dominated by minimally regulated corporations may not be the best way to have a secure future for Canada. It seems reasonable in this period of great economic uncertainty to ask questions about the very nature and assumptions of the American Way of doing business. Clearly, unregulated corporatism has not benefitted most of the American populace very much in recent years. It may be that unregulated corporatism and neoliberalism backed up with American military force are the genuine threats to Canada and Canadians, just as they are to other nations that the United States happens to dislike or distrust at any given moment in time.

The myths of the American version of the market economy have roots in the thinking of Adam Smith and others in the 18th and 19th centuries that saw both the promise and evils of rampant unregulated market economies. Charles Dickens chronicled the evils of early industrialization on workers and the greater British society. The problems with market economies have never been related to their capacity to generate immense wealth. The markets, businesses and corporations in competition with one another do this with great efficiency. Rather, the problems and evils relate

JAMES P. LUDWIG PH.D

to the distribution of the new wealth, the regulation of business practices and how the costs of businesses are externalized to the environment as pollution that damages the larger population and commonweal.

Taxation of created wealth and the redistribution of this largess to programs for all citizens has long been the mechanism in both countries for redistribution of wealth to achieve some level of equity. Environmental regulation and public health programs have been the means to reduce the inequities that accompany the externalized costs of pollution. However, the implementation of neoliberal philosophy has reduced taxes on the wealthy and corporations and crippled all regulation thereby distorting the long-accepted balance between most of the people, business and the environment. The Harper government has now distorted this balance further by reducing the time required to permit new projects, limiting environmental impact reviews to just two years.

The last decade in the United States can been seen accurately as the triumph of the long held principles of neoliberalism that underpin the American version of market economies. Although the roots of this political philosophy lie in the 18th and 19th centuries, the modern version is best represented by the writings of Chicago school of economic thought, particularly the late Milton Freidman. Neoliberal economic theory holds that taxation of the wealthy and corporations should be minimal in order to create pools of wealth for reinvestment; reinvestment will create jobs and benefits will trickle down to all citizens through job creation. Regulation of businesses should be minimal, and government as small as possible with the private sector assuming as many of the traditional functions of government as are profitable to business. And, individuals are encouraged to accumulate as much wealth as possible regardless of the means used and the costs externalized to the environment (Beder, 2008). The American tendency to celebrate individuals over community has rarely been so obvious.

Private business *is claimed* to be more efficient than governments by neoliberals for virtually every function, although there is precious little evidence to prove this assertion. Although this premise has never been tested systematically by unbiased studies that compare the successes and failures of public vs. private enterprises, this belief is trumpeted as loudly by those steeped in neoliberal philosophy as literal interpretations of the

Bible are by fundamentalist Christians. Accumulation of as much wealth as possible is seen to be the cardinal virtue. The individual is to be solely responsible for their place in, and contributions to, society. Governments should be as small as possible so as not to interfere in business that will self-regulate through competition. Business is better-suited to protect the public because it is more efficient than governments that are wasteful. *Take note: Virtually none of these neoliberal economic theories have been shown to be valid.* However, these were the exact philosophical components of the foul soil that nurtured the taproots of the worldwide economic collapse in 2008 (Stiglitz 2010).

Perhaps the most significant of these neoliberal principles is minimal taxation of the wealthy and corporations. The belief that tax cuts for the wealthy and corporations will automatically translate to job creation is a myth. The wealthy tend to save much more of their windfalls than the average person that must spend virtually all of their income to sustain their place and health (Stiglitz op.cit.). This is particularly true in America where health care is a private for profit venture, and well over 40% of Americans do not have an employer willing or able to pay for their health care policies.

Similarly, tax cuts for corporations do not flow directly into job creation, but onto the balance sheet where they are treated usually as profits. Consider the dilemma for the CEO of a corporation. What is important to the CEO is to produce dividends every quarter to be able to attract stockholders to buy more shares, increase their company's stock prices and pay dividends. What does actually 'trickle down' from corporate tax cuts are bonuses to management, rising stock and bond prices and dividends to stockholders. Miss a series of quarterly dividends, and then a CEO will be at risk of loss of his job at worst, or will get no bonus at best. These are serious matters in a culture that promotes individual wealth as the primary goal for a successful person. *All the incentives for the leaders of a business that receives a tax cut are to retain that windfall as earnings on the balance sheet, especially because corporate management is compensated and retained on the basis of current performance for their stockholders. There is absolutely no incentive to create jobs by means of simple tax cuts for businesses.*

Job creation means spending money in the hope that more of the company's products or services can be sold. In a competitive world, that

JAMES P. LUDWIG PH.D

is risky, especially in tough economic times. The safe decision is to hold onto that money as long as possible, especially since a healthy balance sheet translates to bonuses for managers. Interestingly, three years after the 'meltdown' of 2008 in midsummer 2011, American corporations were carrying well over two trillion dollars of cash on their balance sheets. In the 4th quarter of 2012, the world's largest corporation by market value, Apple, had 131 billion dollars on its balance sheet alone. But, unemployment remained stubbornly near 8% of those still looking for work. Nearly 17% of Americans would work if they could just find a job, but had abandoned their searches for work. Similar rates of jobless were present in Canada, especially the Maritimes. And, the very same American banks and investment houses that had orchestrated the meltdown paid their CEOs and executives record bonuses in 2009 and 2010, often from the same bailout funds provided by the American government.

All of this hardship came after thirty years of substantial tax cuts to corporations and the wealthy, coupled with degregulation of markets and banks, especially under the George W. Bush administration. Even with that experience, neoliberal theorists and politicians (especially the Republicans in the US and Conservatives in Canada) continue to demand more tax cuts for corporations and the wealthy, touting the theory that this will induce businesses to create jobs. At municipal levels, many communities have even forgone property taxes on new corporate investments in an attempt to attract new jobs to their region. The primary result has been a race to the bottom in the collection of tax revenues used to fund those public programs that nurture the commonweal.

Regulation of American and Canadian businesses, especially corporations, has been declining inexorably for three decades. The neoliberal mantra that regulations harm businesses became ascendant in the Reagan and Mulroney administrations following the decade of regulatory reform in the 1970s that was the pinnacle of 'the great society' vision of Lyndon Johnson in the US and parallel activities by the Trudeau administrations in Canada. Many long-needed laws to regulate air, water and pesticide pollution, food quality and business practices were passed and supposedly implemented by agencies between 1965 and 1980. Government grew large in both nations. Arguably, there was truth to the neoliberal concern that large deficits incurred by large governments and clumsy new regulations were harmful to business in the near term.

However, those concerns should not have been *carte blanche* to delete all regulatory and pollution controls on business as neoliberal governments are wont to do. Consider the recent Budget Implementation Bill (C-38) introduced in the Canadian Parliament. The Conservative government in a single draconian sweep of its parliamentary majority has wiped out decades of protection for natural resources, the environment and many social programs, justifying these on the alter of presumed efficiencies in economic growth by the private sector for Canada. This is neoliberalism at its very finest: Tilt everything towards businesses and corporations and woe be unto those less fortunate, especially First Nations citizens in Canada, who are trampled in the aftermath. It is reminiscent of Admiral Dewey's infamous comment uttered during the Battle for Manila Bay during the Spanish American War of 1898 'Damn the torpedos, full speed ahead!'

In essence, business was constrained from externalizing the costs of their gross pollution and risky practices to the environment and public during the 1960s and 70s in North America. Unethical business practices, food safety, pesticides, air and water quality all were regulated to protect consumers. Quite suddenly, businesses were required to meet standards of all sorts to protect the quality of the environment and the food they processed. New regulations were imposed on the banking and investment sectors also, especially in America, while Canada continued its very conservative approach to regulating its banks.

American corporations and banks chafed under these changes and set out to capture the political and regulatory communities for their benefit, including providing schools with free 'educational materials' on business that touted the virtues of capitalism and attacked social programs as wasteful government spending (Beder 2008). With so much of Canadian businesses under control of US-based corporations, the same neoliberal strategy to eliminate government regulation soon surfaced in Canada, aided openly by Brian Mulroney who admired Margaret Thatcher and Ronald Reagan to an embarrassing, even worshipful, degree for their promotion of neoliberal corporatism. Enough of the public bought into these arguments to elect increasingly conservative neoliberal politicians in both countries. The result was the virtually complete erosion of monetary regulation and controls on corporations, investment houses and banking in the United States and Great Britain by 2003 that led directly to the economic collapse of 2008. Fortunately, Canada did not allow its banking sector to run amuck and still has a well regulated banking system that is the envy of the developed world today.

A particularly sinister aspect to the ascendency of corporatism since WW II has been the capture of the government agencies by the very corporations they were supposed to be regulating. It is interesting to recall the content of President Dwight Eisenhower's last major speech in December, 1959. His was a stark warning to Americans not to allow industries to capture the US military and create a 'military-industrial' complex that could then set and control American military policy for their narrow economic interests. Arguably the two decade-long conflicts of Viet Nam and the Second Gulf War have been manifestations of exactly what had so troubled 'Ike', the consummate, but thoughtful, warrior of WWII in Europe. In retrospect, Ike's concerns were not surprising after his own secretary of Defense, Charles E. Wilson, had uttered the infamous remark that "What is good for General Motors is good for the country.' just two years earlier. The unfortunate American military adventures of the last forty years—particularly Viet Nam, the Second Gulf War and even Afghanistan—suggest strongly that Ike was right on point and Charlie was dead wrong, plain and simple.

In the investment banking and securities sectors of America's Wall Street, a pattern of the 'revolving door' of regulators between Wall Street and the government's agencies like the Securities and Exchange Commission was condoned, and even promoted by both Republican and Democratic administrations after 1980. Many regulatory laws (e.g. pesticide, food and drug registration legislation) were altered to require that the corporations proposing to use or market a product provide the testing data on the proposed product to the governmental regulatory agencies that were then lobbied to approve the product by the same corporations. Substantially, Canada has the same regulatory structure as the US for health and food safety. Corporations typically provide the test data on which decisions about efficacy and safety are reached in Canada too.

As a scientist, I am keenly aware that you can design tests to find or hide what you want in the results. How you frame the null hypothesis and ask the questions by the tests you perform are supremely important influences on the analyses produced by your work and the probity of those data. It is an act of pure faith to accept that any business with an interest in the outcome of tests will act ethically to produce an unbiased data set and results, always ask the right questions, use the right research methods, run the evaluations long enough and apply the suitable statistical tests. Yet, those are the principle assumptions that structure virtually all regulatory laws in the US and Canada in this neoliberal era. Regulators are supposed to 'review and approve' based on the data supplied by the companies that will then sell whatever product it is they are applying to be approved by the governments.

Consider the stark effects on the commonweal of these examples. In 1959 multinational drug makers pressed the US Food and Drug Administration vigorously to approve thalidomide™, a unique sleeping agent that had been developed and approved for use in Europe in 1958. The FDA refused to license the drug for use in the US based on equivocal animal testing data suggesting possible increases in birth defects in offspring of pregnant animals given the drug. Several multinational drug makers roundly criticized the agency publicly for interference in their businesses, keeping a good new drug from American consumers. Their lobbyists even tried to get the responsible FDA officials that made the decision fired, but the agency held firm. FDA staffers were protected and the drug was never licensed for use in North America.

Within the next two years, over ten thousand European children were born with the birth defect *phocomelia* (a naturally very rare defect of 'flipper-like' arms and legs, resembling the appendages of seals, genus *Phoca*); at least 97% of the European women who birthed these children had taken thalidomide™ as a prescribed sleeping drug. Over the same period in the US, there were 61 cases of phocomelia. All but twelve of these American cases were linked to women who had used thalidomide™ when on vacation, working or living in Europe. I suspect that had this drug been brought to the FDA and Health Canada in 2000, it would have been approved easily in both the US and Canada.

Especially since 1980, with the ascendency of the Reagan and Mulroney administrations that began the concerted process of business and environmental deregulation, there has been a rash of bad drug-related outcomes following the lobbied approvals of new heart, blood pressure, bladder and kidney function medicines that have led to increases in side effect damages and deaths in the US and Canada. Drugs like Avandia™, Vioxx™ and many others have been found to be associated with bad outcomes, usually through side effects on non-target organs, especially among the elderly. Typically, all animal test data that suggested problems might exist were withheld from agencies, dismissed or soft-pedaled by lobbyists for the drug manufacturers as they secured permission to sell each new 'wonder drug'. In some instances, data sets that found side effects, or were equivocal, were never submitted to the regulatory agencies. In other cases, tests were run for periods far too short to find effects, even when the manufacturers' own scientists suspected they were there. The regulators were often complicit by approving new drugs rapidly with far too little, or grossly incomplete, testing in order to appease their corporate critics. As so often happens in organizations, it was 'Go along to get along.' which actually made the public the test animals for these dangerous drugs.

In the food and environmental regulatory areas there are equally troubling graphic instances of agency misconduct at the behest of corporations that Canadian and American agencies were supposed to regulate. Chopra (2009) has documented the capture of Health Canada by corporate interests, particularly Monsanto's promotion of genetically modified foods and plants, and potent substances used to manipulate animals like growth hormones. Chopra even documented an attempt at outright bribery to get the agency to approve bovine growth hormone (BGH). Eventually, Chopra and two other Canadian scientists lost their jobs in 2005 over similar conflicts with the agency administrators as they tried to 'blow the whistle' on agency misconduct. When working in agencies of neoliberal governments, telling the truth can be very dangerous to one's career. Employees understand this; often they simply ignore their agency's mandate in order to retain their jobs and just hope for the best.

The USEPA and Coast Guards of both nations have a dismal record of enforcing the laws and policies related to invasive aquatic species, largely because these agencies refused to enforce the mandates they were assigned under clean water legislation in 1973 to regulate ballast water that is the source of most alien species invading our fresh waters at the behest of the shipping industry (Alexander 2009). In the 36 years after the regulation of ballast water was assigned to the USEPA in 1973, that then passed this assignment on to the US Coast Guard (Canada made a similar decision), 48 new aquatic invasive species appeared in the Great Lakes including zebra and quagga mussels, round and tube-nosed gobies and the ruffe. The three fish species have totally restructured and devastated the native fish communities of the lakes while the mussels have converted the food web of the lake from a pelagic to a benthic ecological system. The mussels have now spread across North America invading most fresh water systems. *The mussel species alone cause an estimated seven billion dollars per year of direct damage to utilities, recreation, and fisheries in the US alone that must be borne and paid for by the public (Alexander, op.cit.). The shipping industry that benefited for four decades from not having to pay for relatively inexpensive means to control invasive species in their ballast waters has paid virtually none of these externalized costs!* We, the public, our environment and native species ecologies pay for this externalized damage instead, while the businesses and corporations of the shipping industries continued to enjoyed a few million of annual savings for several decades. This was not exactly a reasonable cost-benefit tradeoff.

If ever there was an exquisite example of the magnitude of real externalized costs associated with government agencies allowing a form of pollution that was made explicitly against the law, but allowing it anyway, this is it. Once the Coast Guards of the two countries were captured by the shipping corporations they were supposed to regulate, and the USEPA refused to do its duty under the US Clean Water Act, a very bad outcome was virtually assured simply because all decisions on invasive species controls were subordinated to the profitability and convenience of the shipping interests. Moreover, unlike a point source pollution source that effects damage only locally, this example has real 'legs'. These mussels have changed the most fundamental structure of Great Lakes ecological systems and have spread throughout freshwaters continent-wide. The costs to control their deleterious presence will last for decades as a continuous drain on public resources. An ultimate cost of hundreds of billions of dollars over many decades is very likely and the shipping industry was let off scot-free.

Interestingly, no federal employees in either country were dismissed or even chided for their actions as this horrific damage materialized. Instead, agency lawyers in each country protected the agencies and their faulty policies in court cases. The USEPA under George W. Bush fought stubbornly for six years not to be forced to take back the control of invasive species from the US Coast Guard. Only when ordered by the federal courts to do so, did the agency finally accept the responsibility for this regulation in 2008—35 years too late. No appreciable fines have been assessed on the shippers themselves. The basic response by the regulators and their principal oversight agency, the International Joint Commission, has been only to call for stricter controls on invasive species. It has been a classic example of slamming the barn door shut for a second time long after the stallion escaped and fathered a passel of foals! Simply put, there is absolutely no accountability in an unregulated neoliberal world for externalized costs. Moreover, the hollowed out shells of once effective regulatory agencies became as effective a protective barrier to misconduct as does the shed skin protect the snake. They became shells, regulators in name only, abettors of the damage in fact.

Whenever this kind of pernicious influence is allowed to occur under a neoliberal-focused government, the foxes have been granted preferential access to the henhouse (Gore 2007). Then public interest is put at risk and the public is forced to pay for the resultant damage. Essentially, people are being put in the role of experimental animals in the case of premature drug and pesticide approvals, economic and ecological damage were the direct result of the invasive species, and increased risk of environmental diseases (like cancer and thyroid insufficiency) when many industrial pollutants were allowed to persist over a long period of time (Heindel 2010, Braden *et al.* 2006 a. b., Gilbertson and Brophy 2001; Gilbertson and Watterson 2007). Then, the public and our common resources (*the commonweal*) bears all the costs because there are few means to recover damages from the corporations that caused these problems by pollution and agencies cannot be sued for the damages resulting from poor regulation.

Further, it is common that the regulatory bodies hide from public awareness how these things have happened. Most victims of environmental diseases from pollution die long before they could collect damages, and corporations can afford the best lawyers to drag out proceedings for many years. In Canada one has only to look at the four decade long fight of Quebecois workers in the asbestos industries to see how vigorously corporations will fight to continue to pollute regardless of the horrid effects on their workers. For many businesses, workers and wildlife recipients of their pollution are simply another commodity to be fed into their businesses regardless of the actual cost in lives and disease. For these neoliberal entities, the commonweal is just an inconvenience and utterly irrelevant to their bottom line.

Those protections that do exist are legal and are effective only if the lawsuits are won. Lawsuits are expensive and always take a long time to be resolved, during which the misconduct and its damaging effects always continue unabated. Worse, even successful lawsuits rarely solve the root cause of problems that were engendered by irresponsible practices because the damage has accumulated over time and often persists for generations. Often, the really significant economic damage occurs as overburdened health care systems when people get sick or have their potential reduced (Stewart *et al.* 2008, Jacobson and Jacobson 1996). Sometimes property values and whole regions are economically depressed for many years when environmental pollutants are persistent and pernicious. The amount of economic loss can be immense, in the range of hundreds of billions of dollars and exceedingly persistent (Braden *et al.* 2006 a. and b.).

It is interesting to ask who has the incentive to allow these externalized environmental problems to continue and fester as long as possible? The answers are the polluters themselves as they maximize profits. Moreover, often it is in the economic interest of multinational drug companies to make palliative substances to treat the symptoms of environmentally caused illnesses that simply alleviate the pain and suffering of victims, but not to address the root cause of their problems. But, our neoliberal politicians do not ask these questions. Instead they cut corporate taxes indiscriminately and remove as many regulations as possible under the guise of improving economic efficiency. The right economic question to ask is whether having regulatory systems that regulate in name only is more, or less, expensive than treating the disease and tolerating the damage that always plays out in societies that fail to regulate businesses properly.

Externalized costs are anathema to the adherents and practitioners of neoliberal doctrines because some government agency must be paid to guard the public interest. But, effective regulation requires money accumulated from taxes to support agencies and larger governments. Effective regulation is not possible when government is kept as small as possible and the regulated parties have preferential access to their regulators through lobbyists through a revolving door between industry and their regulatory agencies. However, these externalized costs are real and often devastate formerly healthy parts of North America, our native ecologies and all exposed people. The only solace in this dismal picture is this. Some of those who act so irresponsibly by externalizing pollution costs to the environment and the commonweal will develop those same diseases too as they are exposed to the pollutants their corporations have produced, refused to treat and expelled to the environment. That seems a fitting fate.

Similarly, deregulation of American banking and the lax control of Securities and Exchange Commission had horrific effects on the world economies. Stiglitz (2010) chronicled the immense 'Ponzi scheme' that Wall Street investment houses and the American banking system had developed and promoted from the mid-1990s through 2007 based on home ownership. By assuming that home values and real estate prices would always increase and then lending to unqualified buyers as much as 110% of the value of a speculative property, a massive Ponzi scheme was developed with *de facto* US government sanction to secure the investment dollars of millions of people worldwide through massive programs of government assured loans to unqualified American buyers. Worse, through complex derivatives like the infamous credit-default-swaps, the poorly secured debt was syndicated and sold worldwide. This crisis is far from over; yet these actions have destroyed many trillions of dollars of retirement and investment funds worldwide already. More will be lost and inflation will rise devaluing our currencies further before this is finally finished. In part, the 2012 debt crisis in Europe has one prominent root in the US-based 2008 economic debacle that triggered massive government spending to prop up most national economies.

These are the ripened fruits of poor regulation and the neoliberal doctrine of minimal interference in business. The corporate and financial foxes have eaten the eggs and killed many of the hens that laid the golden eggs in our free market economies. It is that simple. If we are to fix this mess, we must change the structure and funding of our government. Most importantly, we must fence the corporate foxes out of our public henhouses. Either we do that, or accept that we prefer to have a neoliberal market-driven economy and society dominated by a privileged few very rich, very fat, very warm and supremely contented foxes while most of us go hungry and cold as we see our modest investments devalued or destroyed. Worse, we all get sicker and die younger when environmental pollutants stimulate responses like increased cancer rates and endocrine disruption in the exposed general population as environmental regulation is destroyed.

Is this what we want for Canada and Canadians? If not, then we must act to change it, and do so very soon. Even if it is too late for our individual interests and health, we must understand that our children are next in the line-up of potential victims. Will Canadians settle for so little in an unregulated neoliberal world? Or will Canadians change their political direction and express their will to put an end these neoliberal policies? Are we a commonwealth that recognizes all Canadians are 'in the same boat' or are we just individuals willing to compete ruthlessly in a neoliberal world where no one cares for their neighbors and friends?

Indeed, what kind of people are we?

JAMES P. LUDWIG PH.D

12

Failing market-driven North American economies and political choices.

HISTORICALLY, WEALTH AND power concentrated in an oligarchic class of an empire's citizens were the seeds of social turmoil, protests and instabilities that led eventually to violent political upheavals and the fall of kingdoms and empires. Athens in fifth century BC, the Roman Empire in the fourth century AD, France in 1789, Cuba in 1958, and many states of the Arab world since 2011 provide powerful examples of the unrest that accompanies the concentration of economic and political power in the hands of oligarchs unresponsive to needs or human rights. Often, the result was violent revolution following of many years of peaceful protest once it was clear the oligarchs would never surrender their privileges or even a small part of their wealth.

The United States seems to have accumulated these dangerous conditions with a very rich economic superclass where 1% of the people have, or control, nearly half the wealth of the nation. It is no stretch to speculate that Americans could find their society increasingly chaotic. The political gridlock of the US since the November, 2010 elections may be only the start of a long period of American political instability that will rattle the economies and politics of all nations frequently. A fundamental question for Canadians is whether it is time to distance their country from the path the United States is on, and search for different means to govern Canada in the 21st century.

Many commentators have noted the complicity of both major political parties in the US as this situation developed. Taxes on corporations and the wealthy were cut by votes of members of both parties after 1980. Loopholes in the very complicated US income tax structure created many opportunities for the wealthy and corporations to avoid taxes and hide income. The fact that Warren Buffett and Mitt Romney pay a much lower tax rate than their secretaries illustrates the disparity vividly. The anti-taxation trend in the US really began with the hyper-capitalism promoted by the Reagan presidency. His administration embraced the neoliberal economic doctrines and theories of the Chicago School of Economics like evangelical converts. The effects of deregulation of businesses on the commonweal have been stark as well. American banks and brokerages were 'freed' of substantial regulation beginning in the Reagan presidency, and aided by subsequent administrations of both parties. Finally, deregulation of the American financial sector was completed by George W. Bush in 2002. The result was the American real estate and housing bubble that saw trillions of dollars lent to people with little or no capability to earn enough to pay back the loans (Stiglitz 2010).

When the inevitable crash occurred in 2008, the worldwide effect was to see between 35 and 45 trillion dollars of accumulated wealth disappear, a burgeoning US government debt, destabilized banks and investment houses and the loss of the reputation of the US as a well managed economy. The world awoke late in 2008 to the fact that Wall Street gurus, bankers and the government regulators—the very scions of American business—'had no clothes', just like the mythical naked emperor. Unfortunate for him, President Obama inherited a monumental mess from his doctrinaire neoliberal Republican predecessor. Unfortunate for us, Mr. Obama has only begun to recognize the extent and pernicious nature of neoliberal doctrines with his second term inaugural speech. But, his first administration was complicit to continue the George W. Bush economic debacle. However, with his background as a community organizer, Mr. Obama does understand the commonweal concept. There is genuine hope that his second administration will address some of the inequities of the neoliberal American economic system, provided the American Congress can be persuaded to accept changes.

Fortunately, Canada did not engage in the fiscal ponzi scheme allowed to flourish in the US. Canadian bank regulators had continued to require

JAMES P. LUDWIG PH.D

our banks to lend no more than 75% of real estate value for conventional mortgages. Moreover, the Canadian tax code does not allow mortgage interest to be deducted from taxable income like the US. Today, the Canadian banks are admired for their soundness and stability. American banks, Wall Street brokerages, other American financial institutions and US regulators are derided and mistrusted. Confidence in the world economic system and the US dollar as the world reserve currency has been eroded to an alarming degree. Indeed, the unbridled greed so characteristic of neoliberal market economies has come with a very steep price for everyone, not just those who lost invested dollars or saw their home values plummet.

The net effect for Americans was that the rich got richer, the poor got poorer and the middle class was forced inexorably to shoulder the economic burdens of American society. It is most interesting how the inheritors of the Reagan/Freidman/Bush/Harper philosophy have morphed the bankrupt theories of neoliberal economics a popular belief that the poor (including First Nations in Canada) are lazy and should be shut out of the American and Canadian dreams. In their view, the poor do not deserve any breaks, but the wealthy do because they have achieved wealth (even if inherited) and thereby have demonstrated their value to society. The neoliberal mantra of 'just go get a job' flies in the face of reality, for there are far too few jobs to supply the demand for work. Worse, most of the jobs that are available pay poorly and very few low-paying American jobs come with any benefits or employer-paid health care. Simply put, America has created an immense underclass of citizens with drastically curtailed 'American dreams'. It should come as no surprise to thoughtful Canadians that a similar disparity of incomes and opportunities is present already in Canada and could become permanent.

How the frustrations attendant to this inequality will play out in the United States remains to be seen. But, it will not be a pretty outcome and could involve outright revolt and even widespread violence at some point. It is possible that the recent student and sympathetic worker unrest in Quebec and the worldwide *Occupy* and *Idle no more* Canadian First Nations movements are simply the start of many protests. One can only hope that their immense frustration will be connected to neoliberalism curtailing their opportunities to earn a decent living in a secure society in both countries.

By the end of the first decade of the 21st century, this was the soil that nourished the frustrations of the middle class and gave rise to the TEA party (Taxed Enough Already) in America. Sadly, the vociferous TEA party wing of the Republican Party in the US continues to spout the discredited Reagan/Freidman neoliberal theory about tax cuts for corporations and the wealthy even though all empirical evidence shows that it is—at the very best—a misguided and ineffective (if not outright pernicious) approach to economic stimulus and job creation. Moreover, by protecting these massive pools of accumulated wealth from taxation, the TEA party advocates prevent the government from collecting the revenues it needs to pay down the US national debt and regain balance—a self-inflicted wound if there ever was one!

One impact of the 911 attack was to give impetus to the deeply embedded religious right in the US that reflexively votes for the most socially and economically conservative candidates. Many conservative American politicians have realized that getting elected means being seen to embrace the religious values of Christian fundamentalism through fear because the Christian fundamentalists tend to vote as a block on issues like abortion they perceive to be moral values. Pick the right combination of religious hot button issues, make allusions to, or statements that incite fear, especially of immigrants and Muslims, and the US right wing politicians know those cynical tactics alone come close to a guarantee of election to office in many regions of America. Then, mix that with the frustrations of the middle and lower classes that have seen their share of the tax burden grow ever greater in the last three decades as job creation dwindled and a fertile soil nourishing the TEA party with its narrow, libertarian, religious and moralistic focus on the success of the individual instead of community was created.

Ironically, the TEA party 'trickle-down' economic theory based on low taxes for the wealthy and corporations serves only to make the plight of many of their adherents worse, for it protects the wealthy and corporations from paying a fair share of taxes. Worse, as part of the fundamentalist religious and libertarian cultures, many in the TEA party see any taxation as a moral issue. Compromise is not possible when taxation for the commonweal is seen as an amoral act by those elected who fail to understand the ramifications of their actions. Many of this ilk rely instead on what they believe to be God's plan or their rigid uncompromising libertarian values. Until now, the American political system was based on

JAMES P. LUDWIG PH.D

the principle of compromise. It once was a cumbersome and slow system, but one that led to balance and fairness through compromise. It no longer works because compromise is no longer possible.

These issues have become the base of the platforms of a whole new generation of demagogues—some spewing economic and social nonsense from their pulpits, some on talk shows and television, and some in political rallies. The result is an unsavory alliance that harms everyone in America economically, destabilizes the US political system and foments deep-seated animosities among the less advantaged. This is the reality of America in 2013 and probably will be for many years to come. A totalitarian takeover of the US government could hardly have done more damage. Arguably, the wealthy and corporations have already accomplished a *de facto* takeover of America abetted by their allies in the TEA party wing of the Republican party by simple political obstruction.

Most interestingly, the American Declaration of Independence and Constitution have specific guarantees of separation of church and state that the Republican fundamentalist right has avoided deftly in spirit and fact through claiming their the first amendment right of free speech, even speech that is demonstrably false, if presented as an 'opinion' or belief. It is revealing to consider that while individuals and religions are specifically protected from state control in both countries (i.e. *freedom of religion*), the state is left vulnerable to religious groups that can usurp the political landscape and process. Apparently, it never occurred to the founding fathers of either nation that organized religions could wield enough political power to hijack the political process as has occurred in America in the last two decades.

Speak untruths long and frequently enough through a compliant media, and many come to believe them. George W. Bush did that masterfully with his pre-war pronouncements on Iraq's military capabilities. Presently, most American's believe that Iraq was the state sponsor of the 911 terrorists and that Saddam Hussein had thousands of weapons of mass destruction. Both were outright lies of cynical invention by the Bush administration, spread through a compliant media that reported them frequently under the guise of 'balanced reporting'. These lies bred widespread irrational fear in most Americans and provided the support Mr. Bush needed for his Iraq War, and Republicans continue to use.

The recent debt ceiling crisis and downgrade of the America's debt rating were an inevitable outcome of the coalescence of the religious and political right into a political block that holds Americans hostage to the failed neoliberal economic theories of their value system. Whether this situation will resolve without significant violence and serious social turmoil in the US is an open question: History suggests that it will not. If domestic violence were to become common in America (and in a nation where almost everyone is armed and dangerous, that seems a likely outcome), then a new tsunami of social instability becomes a real possibility. Were that to happen, that same social tsunami would wash up on Canada. We may soon see the brutal handiworks of a new generation of Timothy McVeigh's on the evening news. Canadians do not need to accept or explain the kinds of schizophrenic moral outcomes like Abu Grahib that attend wars started by politicians seeking easy ways out of domestic economic problems through rampant nationalism and militarism directed offshore. It should be bad enough that our American cousins have to tolerate and explain these matters to the world.

Consider the example of the German Weimar Republic created after WW I to replace the imperial rule of the German Kaisers. The economic chaos of the early 1920s first devalued the Mark, then inflation wiped out the German middle class and the worldwide depression threw a third of German's out of work. Protests and violence emerged as the only means for Germans to vent their anger, followed by the inexorable slide into fascism as people embraced a ruthless demagogue promising to stabilize the nation and provide jobs. Hitler gave the German people exactly that and much more than they bargained for; WWII, the holocaust and tens of millions of civilian deaths followed. Will that be the political path the United States will embrace during the 21st century? That is a good question. Moreover, this question alone should stimulate Canadians to distancing Canada from the US and to evaluate the political trends in their own country accurately and dispassionately to be sure it does not happen here too.

Canada has drifted toward the right in the last decade and increasingly embraces the failed neoliberal economic theories of the Chicago School of Economics. Our Prime Minister is an unabashed advocate of more corporate tax cuts, and leads a party with many members that embrace a strong commitment to fundamentalist Christian religion-based values, strikingly similar to the Republicans and their TEA party wing. Worse, he has demonstrated a level of unsavory political rhetoric and sheer viciousness through American style *ad hominem* attack ads aimed at rival party leaders and candidates rather than ideas that evokes the same disgusted responses as the TEA party style politics has in the US. Canada does not need the horrid experience of Gabby Giffords repeated here after vicious partisan verbal and media-sponsored attacks that are the TEA party's election strategies. If one accepts the idea that our prime minister ought to lead Canada thoughtfully, fairly and decorously, then one might conclude Mr. Harper is an abject ethical failure as Prime Minister.

One of the most problematic aspects in America is the absolute unwillingness of the American Right to reach compromises with the more liberal politicians in America. Is this the kind of politics we want for Canada? Do we want to follow the same patterns of huge tax cuts for the wealthy and deregulation of banking that have so crippled the US economy and bred the savage partisanship now rampant in America, a situation that now threatens to bring down the world economy into new economic doldrums by their 'fiscal cliff' and debt ceiling debates? I cannot force myself to believe Canadians are willing to risk the essence of Canada by following the example of the United States; we should be able to do better for all our people than that.

Mr. Harper continues to propose and flirt with a parallel, privatized two-tier medical system for Canada, even though the Canadian people overwhelmingly support and embrace the Canadian system of universal health care. It is any wonder that many Canadians openly fear what the Harper government is now doing to Canada? Regardless of whether Mr. Harper continues in power, the questions about national direction, tax policy and our relationship to the United States are some of the key policy questions for the remainder of this century. How Canadians answer these questions and our political leaders formulate national policy is ever more pressing, for we cannot afford to get this wrong. There will be no second chance for Canada, especially if neoliberalism continues to prosper in America because a *de facto* fascist America may follow (Hedges 2006).

In truth, no political party in Canada, with the possible exception of the New Democratic Party (NDP), has shown a willingness to consider any alternative political philosophy to neoliberalism for the last three decades.

Many conservatives recoil reflexively when anything containing the word 'liberal' is uttered. Yet, their dominant political philosophy is unvarnished neoliberalism in its most pernicious profit-oriented form. The Liberal Party of Canada has also accepted many of the tenants of neoliberalism, spouting the same nonsense about tax cuts for corporations and allowing the capture of Canadian regulatory agencies by corporate interests during their tenure, albeit more quietly.

Anyone who has followed environmental policy closely after the mid 1980s is fully aware of the inexorable erosion of environmental and health agencies and government-sponsored scientific research in Canada. Presently, many of Canada's scientists in universities are funded by corporations to do research of economic interest to their businesses. Health Canada is fully a captive of those corporations it is supposed to regulate (Chopra, 2009). Canada's federal environmental agencies are mere shells of their incarnations of forty years ago; most are understaffed, poorly funded and virtually dysfunctional. Recent actions by the federal and some provincial governments have reduced the manpower of Canadian regulatory agencies to abysmally low levels. Even worse, many Canadian scientists have found their work suppressed through the Privy Council if their findings contradict or reflect badly on the neoliberal philosophy of the Conservative Party. As a scientist I have to ask whether the Harper government is guided at all by unbiased science, real data or the truth? If not, then it is much closer to a religious cult than a political party and we all should prepare to genuflect toward Ottawa.

Fortunately, the slide into unvarnished neoliberalism has been slower in Canada that the US, but the unmistakable signs of the Conservative Party's commitments to this philosophy are obvious and should be deeply troubling to all thoughtful Canadians. There is nothing progressive that could lead to more socially equitable outcomes in the neoliberal philosophy that drives the Conservatives and influences the Liberals strongly. It may be no accident, but rather the emergence of an alternative political philosophy, that the NDP was so successful in Quebec in the last federal election. Of all provinces, Quebec has a tradition of supporting social programs in search of equity for Quebecers. I suspect that their rejection of both established parties was actually rooted in their long held distrust of neoliberal ideas. Even if Quebecers did not recognize exactly why they voted for NDP candidates, they appear to have sensed the amoral stench of neoliberalism. And, the Quebec political swing towards the NDP may well be a harbinger of fundamental change for the nation, as the recent *Occupy movements,* Quebec student protests, Idle no More and similar actions worldwide suggest as well. The fact that the middle classes and youth are becoming engaged in these political actions suggests a monumental backlash against the damages of neoliberalism to their aspirations for a good life is beginning to gather steam. If true, then these movements are likely just the beginning of a new tidal wave of protests that could last a decade or more, similar to the 1960s. Indeed, we live in interesting times!

Of all the Canadian governments' commitments to the commonweal, it is universal health care that is most appreciated and valued. The leadership that culminated in the national decision to adopt universal health care came from the prairie populist Tommy Douglas of the NDP in the 1950s. Douglas believed passionately that health care should be a responsibility of government. Long derided by American commentators as 'socialized medicine', the wisdom of the Douglas vision has been proven by superior performance of the Canadian universal system over more than five decades culminating in better health outcomes, longer lives and much lower costs compare to the private-for-profit US health care model. It can now be judged accurately as a prominent Canadian strength with important benefits to both the individual and businesses.

Other strengths are not as obvious, but every bit as important. Quite surprisingly, in spite of the weak federal system of regulation for securities and corporations, the Canadian banking system stands out as the world's best; this is an incalculably valuable asset to Canadians. Compared to the speculative American and undercapitalized European banking sectors, the well-managed Canadian banks stand forth as a beacon of intelligent management.

As I was composing the first drafts this tract in the summer of 2011, Jack Layton succumbed to cancer. Although I have never supported an NDP candidate and even often dismissed Jack's political ideas with an amused sort of detachment, I was astonished at how bereft I felt at his passing, and even more so by the nearly universal outpouring of grief and sympathy by all Canadians, regardless of their political stripe. I had been struggling to find a means to express what was wrong with Canadian politics without seeming to be wholly negative about the trends. Then Jack's last letter to Canadians appeared. In an instant it was obvious that Jack had figured it out far better than I. Here is the optimistic text of that famous letter of inspiration:

August 20, 2011 Toronto, Ontario

Dear Friends,

Tens of thousands of Canadians have written to me in recent weeks to wish me well. I want to thank each and every one of you for your thoughtful, inspiring and often beautiful notes, cards and gifts. Your spirit and love have lit up my home, my spirit, and my determination.
Unfortunately my treatment has not worked out as I hoped. So I am giving this letter to my partner Olivia to share with you in the circumstance in which I cannot continue.

I recommend that Hull-Aylmer MP Nycole Turmel continue her work as our interim leader until a permanent successor is elected.

I recommend the party hold a leadership vote as early as possible in the New Year, on approximately the same timelines as in 2003, so that our new leader has ample time to reconsolidate our team, renew our party and our program, and move forward towards the next election.

A few additional thoughts:

To other Canadians who are on journeys to defeat cancer and to live their lives, I say this: please don't be discouraged that my own journey hasn't gone as well as I had hoped. You must not lose your own hope. Treatments and therapies have never been better in the face of this disease. You have every reason to be optimistic, determined, and focused on the future. My only other advice is to cherish every moment with those you love at every stage of your journey, as I have done this summer.

To the members of my party: we've done remarkable things together in the past eight years. It has been a privilege to lead the New

JAMES P. LUDWIG PH.D

Democratic Party and I am most grateful for your confidence, your support, and the endless hours of volunteer commitment you have devoted to our cause. There will be those who will try to persuade you to give up our cause. But that cause is much bigger than any one leader. Answer them by recommitting with energy and determination to our work. Remember our proud history of social justice, universal health care, public pensions and making sure no one is left behind. Let's continue to move forward. Let's demonstrate in everything we do in the four years before us that we are ready to serve our beloved Canada as its next government.

To the members of our parliamentary caucus: I have been privileged to work with each and every one of you. Our caucus meetings were always the highlight of my week. It has been my role to ask a great deal from you. And now I am going to do so again. Canadians will be closely watching you in the months to come. Colleagues, I know you will make the tens of thousands of members of our party proud of you by demonstrating the same seamless teamwork and solidarity that has earned us the confidence of millions of Canadians in the recent election.

To my fellow Quebecers: On May 2nd, you made an historic decision. You decided that the way to replace Canada's Conservative federal government with something better was by working together in partnership with progressive-minded Canadians across the country. You made the right decision then; it is still the right decision today; and it will be the right decision right through to the next election, when we will succeed, together. You have elected a superb team of New Democrats to Parliament. They are going to be doing remarkable things in the years to come to make this country better for us all.

To young Canadians: All my life I have worked to make things better. Hope and optimism have defined my political career, and I continue to be hopeful and optimistic about Canada. Young people have been a great source of inspiration for me. I have met and talked with so many of you about your dreams, your frustrations, and your ideas for change. More and more, you are engaging in politics because you want to change things for the better. Many of you have placed your trust in our party. As my time in political life draws to a close I want to share with you my belief in your power to change this country and this world. There are great challenges before you, from the overwhelming nature of climate change to the unfairness of an economy that excludes so many from our collective wealth, and the changes necessary to build a more inclusive and generous Canada. I believe in you. Your energy, your vision, your passion for justice are exactly what this country needs today. You need to be at the heart of our economy, our political life, and our plans for the present and the future.

And finally, to all Canadians: Canada is a great country, one of the hopes of the world. We can be a better one—a country of greater equality, justice, and opportunity. We can build a prosperous economy and a society that shares its benefits more fairly. We can look after our seniors. We can offer better futures for our children. We can do our part to save the world's environment. We can restore our good name in the world. We can do all of these things because we finally have a party system at the national level where there are real choices; where your vote matters; where working for change can actually bring about change. In the months and years to come, New Democrats will put a compelling new alternative to you. My colleagues in our party are an impressive, committed team. Give them a careful hearing; consider the alternatives; and consider that we can be a better, fairer, more equal country by working together. Don't let them tell you it can't be done.

My friends, love is better than anger. Hope is better than fear. Optimism is better than despair. So let us be loving, hopeful and optimistic. And we'll change the world.

All my very best,
Jack Layton

Inspiring words come in many guises—speeches, books, essays, fiction, aphorisms and folk sayings among others. Jack's letter is a modern classic of commentaries written by Canadians. He asks for our best behavior in politics and our commitments to redress what is wrong, or less than ideal, in Canadian affairs. While there is an obvious political message in the content, the Layton letter is far more accurately read as an appeal to our

JAMES P. LUDWIG PH.D

better selves by a dying politician who loved his country. I suspect it was the combined pathos of his untimely death and the recent unprecedented successes of his NDP party that brought so many Canadians to tears and deep grief over his death whether they knew the man, embraced his ideas and politics, or not. I cannot believe that the current leaders of Canada's other political parties would stimulate such genuine grief and emotion were they to die unexpectedly. That alone says a lot.

So what do we have to change about Canadian politics? First, I suggest the recent dismal slide into American attack politics directed at persons rather that ideas must be restrained or utterly rejected. The tendencies of the Canadian Right to emulate the American Right's willingness to destroy their opponents by innuendo and false charges leveled against leaders by *ad hominem* attacks rather than engaging in debates of ideas and concepts should be rejected by Canadians. Jack showed us a better way. We may not have agreed with Jack's political ideas and philosophies, but we all responded to his optimism and fairness in the political campaigns he led. He rejected 'attack ads' and argued for his ideas and policies, even when his concepts seemed to be naïve and possibly uneconomic. I suspect the next election will expose further the despicable present practices of personal attacks, intentional misleading of voters (e.g. the robocall scandal), and politics of fear in Canadian politics. I hope fervently that Canadians will remember Jack's example and reject those using them.

Stephen Harper, are you capable of hearing Jack's words? Do you understand the morass of negativity you and the Conservative Party have led Canadian politics into by emulating the American political rhetoric, methods of the ad hominem *attack and outright lies? Shame on you! Canada deserves better in its political discourse. Show us that kind of caring, enlightened personal leadership demonstrated by Jack or begone from Canadian politics! Your behavior and that of your minions is often just disgusting.*

Liberals, can you forswear the divisive politics now rampant in the American electoral and legislative system that the Conservatives are importing to Canada? Are you capable of reconsidering your flirtation with, and commitments to, neoliberalism? Or, will you continue to be like the Democrats in America and 'talk the talk', but refuse to 'walk the walk'? As you choose a new leader, consider not only the immediate goal of recapture of power, but the longer term impacts of your policies on the commonweal and the needs of all Canadians.

NDPers, have you elected a leader in Thomas Mulcair who is similar to Jack with the lack of hubris but less of the 'common touch' we all loved and appreciated deeply in Jack? And now, can you select, promote and implement those responsible social and environmental policies that will benefit the commonweal? Canada needs exactly that at this moment in our history. That defines your challenge as you aspire to form a new government for Canada. You can succeed if you grasp this, but you will fail if you do not.

JAMES P. LUDWIG PH.D

13

Ways to direct and participate in beneficial changes for Canada.

SO, HOW DOES the average Canadian actually participate in the process of choosing new directions for Canada rather than being dragged along passively with the general flow of our society? I submit that the process of change begins with a clear understanding of what can be changed and what cannot. Obviously, one can change lifestyle, philosophy or politics, but most natural events and climate are very likely beyond one's influence.

Even so, many of the things we cannot change directly, we can have at least a small influence upon. For example, if we lessen the use of fossil fuel energy we will have a very tiny impact on carbon dioxide emissions and a commensurate miniscule effect on the pace of climate change. But, nothing we can do will influence when and where the next earthquake happens in Canada. What follows is my list of the major things we can do as individuals to influence the pace and direction of the changes coming to Canada beneficially.

- Do everything we can to restore to and enhance civility in politics of Canada. We should insist that our leaders restrict debates to ideas and policies and leave the personal attack politics to the Americans. Canadians must not allow our politics to slip further into the morass of evil confrontations and mudslinging that has so thoroughly paralyzed American politics and their Republic style of democracy. Admittedly, politics is a very rough game, but then so are Canadian football and hockey. We have devised means to make those fair contests with officials that regulate the games fairly. We, the Canadian citizens, must regulate political games with our votes. *We are the referees of the games of governments and politicians; it is long overdue that we take on that role seriously.*

- Insist that our leaders convene a national conversation and commission on the future of the Canadian north. Canada's larger future is linked inextricably the way we go about development there. The opportunities in this region are as great as they are challenging. The potential rewards for the nation and all Canadians are immense and must not be wasted. A national conversation on the best means to capitalize on these opportunities is long overdue; that does not mean the unleashing of unregulated development there. Canada cannot develop a reasonable vision of the future unless developing the north properly is at the core of our national agenda. Addressing the long avoided problems for First Nations must be integral to these efforts.

- Insist that the Prime Minister and all political leaders contribute to a national panel with members from the provinces, the scientific community and interest groups to understand the probable effects of climate change and plan for that based on the best science available. For the better part of two decades the Liberals gave climate change lip service but did little of substance, while the Conservatives largely chose to discredit the science as 'unsettled'. The time for delay and obfuscation is past. Climate change is the most important trend of the 21st century and probably the 22nd as well. Canadians deserve a civil conversation on the topic, *underpinned by the best science available* to be able in order to galvanize the electorate to accept and contribute to the solutions to the immense suite of problems that climate change will inflict on Canada. The climate is changing with increasing speed. No one can stop it. We cannot avoid the consequences. But, we can slow it down if we choose to. And, we can take advantage of the opportunities presented to us by climate change once we understand it.

- Insist that the Prime Minister commit the nation and allow access to the best science available to guide public policy. In the last six

JAMES P. LUDWIG PH.D

years, the Harper government has systematically moved to muzzle dissenting or contrarian voices in the greater scientific community. All government scientists must now vet their work through the Privy Council, a political body in control of government policy. Scientists that gather data or make analyses not supportive of Conservative aims or neoliberal policies are being dispensed with; their science is being hidden from the Canadian public. Politicians are ill equipped with the sophisticated scientific background to understand most technical issues and have zero inclination to admit choices or studies into any conversation that may harm their party philosophy or neoliberal leanings. It is time to pry the lid off suppressed science and return to the use of verified scientific studies to inform public policy rather than allowing political philosophies to control the use and dissemination of new science and findings. Although much worse under the Harper Government, this is not a new problem in either Canada or the US. It has occurred under both Liberal and Conservation Canadian governments, and Republican or Democratic American administrations for decades (Ludwig 1995, Gore 2007, Chopra 2009). However, the Harper led Conservatives have been the most suppressive of new science of all recent administrations in Canada or the US. Canadians must insist that science inform public policy instead of political philosophy or corporate money dictating what is policy.

• Insist that Canada have a thorough public conversation on its place in the world and how we use our small Canadian Forces military, particularly overseas. A large part of what is needed is how we relate our military to the goals and demands of the US. Canada must never fall into the role of an American lackey, deferring to the US on the key military and security matters. Once our role overseas is understood and military policy clarified, then we should consider how to use and enhance our military forces for domestic goals. This should be used to determine which military procurements we really need (e.g. Arctic capable ships and supply aircraft) and those we do not (e.g. F-35 fighter jets). The truth is that we have no international enemies to fight, unless we pick the fight ourselves. And, remember the two oceans plus the vastness of the Arctic do give us substantial protection from all nations except the US.

- Insist on a review of NAFTA and our trading partnership with the US. Clearly, Americans want it 'both ways'—to insulate their markets from Canadian competition, yet have unfettered access to our resources (particularly energy commodities) and the Canadian market. The US is an easy market for Canada to export commodities to, but may not be our most dependable trading partner for the long term. Simply put, Americans adhere to NAFTA only when it is in their self-interest. American money influences Canada's boardrooms, tax policies, even health care significantly. How much American influence is sound policy is a very delicate question, but one that we cannot avoid. Canadians need to make a candid judgment on whether America will be a good friend and trading partner at the end of this century. The high dependency of Canada on the US importing our commodities is likely to be increasingly dangerous over the long term, especially if America lurches further to the Right because American Fascism will be lurking in the nearest political sewer. Canada must find alternative trading partners.

- Insist on a conversation about the degree we are willing to adhere to the 'fortress North America' mindset of the Americans. Thus far, Canada has largely acquiesced to the idea of a common border, but I suggest this is a dangerous policy if we cannot trust American motives completely. As a dual citizen, I have strong doubts that we can. American presidents use military sledgehammers and deliver on veiled threats when their rhetoric fails to cajole others to follow American policies. Moreover, we must not allow Canada to be drawn into a paranoid American worldview that projects their Monroe Doctrine worldwide. There is ample reason to believe that we are worse off for participation in most offshore conflicts and that we do precious little good for those we are there ostensibly to protect by being a part of these military efforts.

- Finally, we must restore a vision that the commonweal and community of Canada are far more important than the selfish interests of the individual or businesses. In truth, we are all in this world together and we must resume acting first for the common good, relegating the interests of the individual and businesses to

JAMES P. LUDWIG PH.D

second place. Every individual and business entity depends on the resources we have in common—our air, water, public lands and publicly-owned resources. We cannot continue to allow some of us preferential access to, or damaging emissions to, the resources of the commonweal. Our health, especially our children's health depends on this more than anything else we accomplish.

Resolution of many of the matters and addressing the opinions presented in this book-length essay require strong leadership by Canada's Prime Minister. Mr. Harper will find this exceptionally difficult since he has embraced with complete devotion the very neoliberal politics and principles that now threaten to unhinge our economy and Canadian society as neoliberalism has done so graphically to the United States. Capitalism has brought us many economic benefits: but, unregulated capitalism threatens to destroy our democracies in the West as rot from the inside. A pungent Sicilian aphorism is appropriate here: 'The fish rots from the head down'. Harper has shown a willingness to suppress the scientific community and others who disagree with his corporatist view of Canada and has acquiesced to the Americans on almost every matter and issue of real substance. The historic antipathy of the Conservatives toward meaningful climate change policies that might have slowed the progress of the impending changes has shown his commitment to business interests first, the Canadian people last. There is great symbolic significance in the Conservative decision to withdraw from the Kyoto Accord, even though this was a flawed approach to worldwide greenhouse gas emissions.

However, it is the people who get the leaders they deserve when they fail to understand what political philosophies actually drives the politicians they elect and flow passively with the herd. The future of Canada and Canadians will not be driven by intelligent policies unless we, the Canadian people, insist on appropriate governance. If we want better leadership, then we have to find the way to nurture, elect and secure it. We can begin by electing people who will do what is right for the commonweal. Most of the current crop of politicians is simply too damn comfortable where they are to go looking for a better path forward. But, with their guaranteed gold-plated pensions why should we expect otherwise?

My intent has not been to deride the United States, but to identify what is wrong with our relationship with America, to show how these problems developed between my countries and the political myths and philosophies that drive each nation toward their fate. I can only hope that this tract is seen not as anti-American, but rather as pro-Canadian. My intent has been to focus Canadians' attention on the far horizon of the dawning of the 22nd century, discussing how we can get there most effectively, efficiently and ethically, even as we must address what is happening in the real world outside of our control. Americans are going to have to find their own path out of their troubles. I wish those living in my birth country well, but have no desire to participate in their roiling neoliberal society that creates so much damage to those with less than the most-wealthy one percent of their population. Most of all, I have wanted to speak plainly of the risks to Canada if we follow their path.

It can be a wonderful journey for Canada if we just get the policies right and do that soon. Then we can find the path to a better, more just and equitable Canada. Our most fundamental duty is to keep **'our true north wild and free',** and do that without **'the rockets' red glare and bombs bursting in air'**.

Time's a wasting my fellow Canadians so let us be about that now!

REFERENCES, CITATIONS & SOURCES.

Adams, M. 2003. **Fire and Ice: The US and Canada and the myth of converging values.** Penguin Books. 224 pp.

Alexander J., 2009. **Pandora's Locks.** Michigan State University Press, East Lansing.

Beder, Sharon. 2008. The Corporate Assault on Democracy. *The International Journal of INCLUSIVE DEMOCRACY*, Vol. 4, No.1.

Braden, J. B., L. O. Taylor, D. Won, N. Mays, A. Cangelosi and A. A. Patunru. 2008a. Economic benefits of remediating the Buffalo River, New York Area of Concern. *Journal of Great Lakes Research* **34**: 631-648.

Braden, J. B., D. Won, L. O. Taylor, N. Mays, A. Cangelosi and A. A. Patunru. 2008b. Economic benefits of remediating the Sheboygan River, Wisconsin Area of Concern. *Journal of Great Lakes Research* **34**: 649-660.

CHCF 2011. California Health Care Foundation. US Health Care Spending 2011. *www*

Chopra, S. 2009. **Corrupt to the Core.** KOS publishing, Caledon, ON. ISBN 978-0-9731945-7-9. 340pp.

CIHI, 2011. Canadian Institute for Health Information, 2011. Health care in Canada 2011. *www.*

Comparison of the health care systems in Canada and the United States. *Wickipedia, www.*

OCED, 2011. Comparing U.S. Healthcare Spending with Other OECD Countries. Organization for Economic Cooperation and Development, *OCED Health Data, 2009. www.*

Gilbertson, M. O. and A. E. Watterson. 2007. Diversionary reframing of the Great Lakes Water Quality Agreement. *Journal of Public Health Policy* **28**: 201-215.

Gilbertson, M. O., and J. Brophy. 2001. Community health profile of Windsor, Ontario: Anatomy of a Great Lakes Area of Concern. *Environmental Health Perspectives* **109** Supplement 6: 827-843.

Gilbertson, M. O. 2009. Index of congenital Minimata Disease (CMD) in Canadian areas of concern in the Great Lakes. *Environmental Toxicology and Chemistry.*

Gore, A. 2007. **The Assault on Reason.** Penguin Press. ISBN 978-1-59420-122-6. 308 pp.

Hedges, C. 2006. **American Fascists: The Christian Right and the War on America**. Free Press, Simon & Schuster, Inc. New York. ISBN-13: 978-0-7432-8443-1. 254 pp.

Heindel, J. 2010, The developmental origins of disease: Environmental pharmaceuticals and epigenetic mechanisms. Presentation to Guelph Conference on Pharmaceuticals and epigenetic mechanisms of diseases. February 27, 2010, Guelph, Ontario.

Jacobson, J. L. and S. W. Jacobson. 1996. Intellectual impairments in children exposed to polychlorinated biphenyls *in utero. New England Journal of Medicine* **335**: 783-789.

Ludwig, J. P. 1995. Science, research, and public policy in the Great Lakes: Making science subservient to politics on IJC boards. [Invited editorial] *Journal of Great Lakes Research* **21**: 159-160.

Schantz, S.L., D.M Gasior, E. Polverejan, R.J. McCaffery, A.M. Sweeney, H.E.B. Humphrey, and J.C. Gardiner. 2001. Impairments of memory and learning in older adults exposed to polychlorinated biphenyls via consumption of Great Lakes fish. *Environmental Health Perspectives* **109**: 605-611.

Stewart P. W.E. Lonky, J. Reihman, J. Pagano, B.B. Gump, and T. Darvill. 2008. The relationship between prenatal PCB exposure and intelligence (IQ) in 9-Year-Old Children. *Environmental Health Perspectives* **116:** 1416-1422.

Visser, M. E. 2007. **Cold Clear and Deadly**. Michigan State University Press. East Lansing.

·

Edwards Brothers Malloy
Thorofare, NJ USA
March 28, 2013